Letting Go

LETTING GO

Robert Lindsay

THOROGOOD

First published in 2009 by
Thorogood Publishing Ltd
10-12 Rivington Street
London EC2A 3DU
Telephone: 020 7749 4748
Fax: 020 7729 6110
Email: info@thorogoodpublishing.co.uk
Web: www.thorogoodpublishing.co.uk

A CIP catalogue record for this book is available
from the British Library.

HB ISBN 978-185418606-5
PB ISBN 978-185418688-1

Book designed and typeset in the UK by Driftdesign

Printed in the UK by Ashford Colour Press

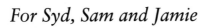

For Syd, Sam and Jamie

ACKNOWLEDGEMENTS

To my family – the real one!

Letting Go is dedicated to the members of my real family, past and present, who have all contributed – directly or indirectly – to this book. Special thanks must go to my wife Rosie who has had to bear the brunt of all the mood swings that make up my personality.

Writing this book has been a longish process (you might almost say it has taken me all my life, so far!). In its preparation I have been hugely helped by Anna de-Pol, my tireless and understanding PA. I would also like to acknowledge the role of my publishers, Thorogood; in particular the help and encouragement of my old friend Neil Thomas and the support of the editorial team of Angela Spall, Andrew Whittaker and Cheryl Wallis.

Inevitably this book has concentrated on me and writing it has certainly been a cathartic experience and even fun (in parts!). But I have become so much more aware throughout the project of all the significant world events that have taken place since 1949 – the incredible political shifts, the conflicts, the assassinations, the amazing changes in society and technology – which have combined to create the world in its current state. I acknowledge, humbly, that in this book, none of that features – it is as if so much was going on in my life that I must have missed something!

*'Think of the trees and how simply they let go,
let fall the riches of a season, how without grief
(it seems) they can let go... Learn to lose in order
to recover, and remember that nothing stays
the same for long... Let it go.'*

May Sarton

CONTENTS

PROLOGUE

MILLENNIUM NIGHT, 31 December 1999: new hope, new expectations, New Labour, new decade for me (I had been fifty on 13 December 1999), new son (Sam, born the month before on 18 November 1999) and great excitement.

I don't like that time of year – I never have. It's just something I feel about New Year's Eve: it is over-hyped and I've always wanted to shy away from the celebrations. I suspect most people feel the same, don't they?

New Year's Eve is a curious mix of nostalgia, a sense of great expectation, and a strong desire to party. But in fact I would much rather sit in my own home and reflect on what has happened to me over the past year. If you have any form of split personality, like me, New Year's Eve is a heady cocktail. I always feel obliged to be merry and celebrate, but invariably I'm reflective and dark. Perhaps this is a 'northern' thing – I've always felt that there is a price to pay for partying; the more fun, the bigger the price. Forget being northern, maybe it's just my age!

Millennium Night was that sort of night. It turned out to be as taxing for me as it seemed to be for the whole nation: the disaster of the Dome, the supposed 'river of fire' on the Thames that was more of a damp squib – it all made me want to sit down and wallow in the nostalgia of my life.

Nostalgia? Baggage more like!

Or so it seemed that night to me: a born-again dad of fifty, the weekend father to an eleven-year-old daughter, and a man still deeply troubled by the break-up with her mother – a relationship blighted by my reaction to an earlier marriage that hadn't worked out. I was in love with my new partner, but was fearful of yet another mistake and was reluctant to commit myself – an attitude that recurs many times in this book. My career could only be described as a rollercoaster ride – up one minute, down the next, one minute comedy, one minute tragedy, here a Shakespeare, there a sitcom.

My split personality really seemed to collide with the year 2000. I've never kept a diary; I've never really felt the need to. I thought I'd always remember everything, but of course you don't. However, something happened on that Millennium Night that would bring back fragmented memories of childhood that I will try to piece together as a jigsaw of my life.

More importantly, it would make me realise that I had been haunted by one particular incident that would affect not only my career but my personal relationships; something that perhaps gave me the wrong attitude to women and made it difficult for me to trust – not only my partners but myself.

Up until that point, I'd lived a life almost in denial. I was self-obsessed and ambitious to the degree that my career was everything. I assumed that somehow the other parts of my life would take care of themselves. Well, they don't. Life is everything and a good career should only enhance a good life. My parents had been married for over fifty years and I suppose I'd always assumed I would enjoy the same longevity with a partner. Whether my failure to do so is a sign of the times or the result of an all-consuming career is a matter of opinion. Whatever the case, I now see that the two things – relationships and career –

need exactly the same attention.

I rang my dad on Millennium Night to celebrate the fact that I was fifty, that he had a new grandson and that it was about to be the next century. "Did you ever imagine that you'd be celebrating the birth of a grandson on the eve of a new century or imagine that you'd have a son of fifty?" I asked. He replied with the immortal line, "Listen, I never imagined I'd be sleeping with a seventy-year-old woman either!.."

It was during the course of the subsequent phone conversation with my mother that she had a heart attack and fell to the ground. I could hear her calling for my dad and I was calling out to her. The phone hit the floor and no one was listening to me. Then the phone went dead. I looked around and my wife Rosie was standing there with a bag saying, "Go now. Just go."

The journey I set off on was from my home near London to Glenfield Hospital in Leicester, because that's where I assumed she would be taken from my parents' home in Stanley Street, Ilkeston. She had been treated at Glenfield Hospital six or seven years before for a bypass operation, which she had miraculously survived. With true Stevenson exaggeration, she had announced to all her friends and family that the doctors had told her she'd had the 'biggest aneurism in Leicestershire'. Why she should boast about having that condition God only knows, but at least she thought that she was Number One.

It was on the way to the hospital – a ninety-minute, near spiritual journey – that I made some kind of contact with my mother. So many forgotten thoughts came back to me, reminiscences of my life and my career – a real mishmash of events.

When I got to the hospital they said, "Joyce, your son Robert's here." She pulled off the oxygen mask, looked deep into my eyes, gave us a huge smile – as if embracing the whole family – and died.

The events of that traumatic night acted like a catalyst for writing this book. The car dash with its rush of random memories, the idea of the generation moving on – it all mingled with those thoughts that you start to have as you get older – particularly at New Year – when you begin to reflect on your life. You see pieces of your own life in the context of your parents' lives and belatedly begin to understand them a bit more, especially as you see your own children – the next generation – growing up, moving on, letting go.

May 2009
Robert Lindsay Stevenson

ONE

TB OR NOT TB?

I'VE STRUGGLED to come to terms with the loss of my mother. I've been reluctant to 'let go'. Curiously enough, in her own life she had the same difficulties when it came to 'letting go', when it came to moving on.

My mother was a huge influence on my life, a very dominant influence, and the only person in the family who showed any, well let's say, artistic temperament. She was mad as a hatter actually. I have treasured memories of her trying to 'let go'. There was her leaving me on the first day of school when I was five, again on the first day at Clarendon College when I was sixteen and then on the day at the station when I left for RADA in 1968. Those, for my mother, were all 'letting go' moments.

She took me to Clarendon College on the Midland General B2 bus to Canning Circus in Nottingham and then we walked together through Pelham Avenue Cemetery, which seemed like the biggest cemetery in England to me. It stretched as far as the eye could see, containing entire previous generations. We walked all the way through it, back up onto Carlton Road and Arnold

Road. Then I made her get on the bus to go back into Nottingham. I remember waving to her and I saw her wipe her eye – the tears of 'letting go'.

My sister, Lorraine, says that Mum died when I got to the hospital in Leicester because she had waited for all of us to be there together. She believes that Mum was reaching out to me spiritually, saying "get here!" and reminding me during my car journey of the incidents of childhood and our early life together – before 'letting go' once and for all. Almost like *she* was recalling moments between us to keep her going, and that those thoughts were transferred directly from her to me. Lorraine inherited my mother's spirituality and has no fear of discussing such things openly – but that's my sister for you.

Tiny, tiny memories were spliced together on that car journey on Millennium Night, most of them of the familiar things that come to mind like family outings and picnics. Others had lain dormant – forgotten – for years. I saw myself coming home from school on one awful occasion when I was told I had pleurisy and pneumonia. That would have been about 1957. I could see myself walking from Kensington School down Nottingham Road back to my house – really, really ill. I'd been sent home because I couldn't breathe. It was a struggle to walk because of this dreadful pain in my side. Little did I know it at the time, but I would end up being sent to a sanatorium with TB of the lung.

Because of the fear of the word – or the letters – 'TB', I was told for years that I'd had pleurisy and pneumonia. Only recently, on a visit to my doctor for a scan, did I discover the truth. The doctor mentioned that I had an old TB scar. "No, no, no. I had pleurisy and pneumonia as a child," I said. The doctor graciously begged my pardon but confirmed that actually it was a TB scar.

Back then, of course, parents didn't talk about those kinds of things and certainly not about putting you in a sanatorium. I was rushed off to hospital and then ended up in the sanatorium in Longfield Lane for twelve weeks. My parents came to see me most evenings. It was during a really hot summer, and I remember hearing all the other kids playing outside. There was a big, big garden at the back where they had lots of parties for the children.

Every Friday I had blood taken from my thumb. It was horrible. I can still feel it now and shudder at the very thought of it. On Monday mornings I was taken to the local hospital in town for an X-ray, which in those days was quite a big thing, quite a novelty.

My dad bought me a Dinky fire engine whilst I was there – the kind of thing that would be a collectors' piece now, or would be if I hadn't promptly taken off its two little bells and pushed them up my nose. They got stuck and I was rushed off to Nottingham Hospital to have them removed. How's that for boredom?

As far as I was concerned, I was in a hospital. It was only when I was in my early forties that I realised that I had actually been in a sanatorium. There was a little boy in the bed next to me who had one of those globes that you shook and it snowed. He and the other kids used to go out to play in the orchards and go to the garden parties, but I was too ill – instead I was wheeled out onto the balcony so that I could see and hear all the other kids playing. While I was on the balcony I took his little toy apart. Well, actually, I cracked it and all the water went "sssssss". All the snow came out, leaving this little figure inside, probably gulping for air a bit like me with my TB. I got into serious trouble for that and duly tried to lie my way out of it.

"I don't know how it happened," I said. "Some man came in and dropped it." A likely story.

I was always a bit of a dreamer as a child and I wonder now what effect those twelve weeks in the sanatorium must have had on me. It was a long time for a child of that age to be more or less on their own, separated from their parents and in an alien environment. It was an isolating experience for me, even though I was used to being on my own as I was an only child for quite a chunk of my childhood.

I was born Robert Lindsay Stevenson on 13 December 1949 at 5 Larklands Avenue in Ilkeston (or Ilson as the locals say), a Derbyshire town clustered around the ironworks (which employed most of my family – even me for a spell as a sewer cleaner).

In my more affected moments, I always inform people that I come from Derbyshire, giving them an image of rolling hills and windswept moors when, in fact, Ilkeston lies just feet away from Nottinghamshire, four miles from the former coal mining town of Eastwood, and doesn't possess anything remotely romantic – apart from the aspirations of its forty thousand inhabitants. It had, and still does have, a great sense of community; its people are open and friendly and not taken to putting on airs and graces. But the manicured front gardens of my childhood have now been paved over; many of its streets, crescents and avenues have become car parks; and, since the demise of the town's industries, alcohol and drugs have taken their toll on the young, many of whom are single parents. This is perhaps, like most observations, rather generalised but my father has watched these changes happen and, in his isolated later years, he sits and reflects – with some bewilderment – on what has happened since the war to the town he has lived and worked in for eighty-four years. I grew up there, the son of Norman and Joyce – a joiner and a cleaner – who were, I was going to say simple, but no, they were, in their own way, quite complicated people. They had no particular aspirations other than bringing up the family and staying together, a code of conduct that seems quite outdated now.

My parents met when Dad was working as a bus conductor. He tells the story of my mother running after the bus one morning and of him helping her aboard. She grabbed his hand as she jumped onto the bus and he said to himself, 'I'm going to marry that woman.'

They were happily married with three children but had much to deal with in their early lives. Illness in my father's life and the loss of his elder brother, Cyril, in the last days of the war (my dad himself had been on one of the first boats into Arromanches during the D-Day landings) had brought a dark edge to his character. But he always was (and still is) down-to-earth, very left wing and a solid Labour man. He used to be a loyal *Daily Mirror* reader, even if it did end up on a hook in our outside lavatory. Nowadays, he refuses to read *any* newspaper so it's back to the old Izal for him! Mum had a real *joie de vivre* and was invariably fun to be with. She was a mystic, and she took great delight in telling fortunes and speaking to the spiritual world, the 'other side'. She would probably have been burnt at the stake in the Middle Ages as she practised a witchcraft of sorts. She read palms and had a crystal ball, which was kept in the understairs larder away from the eyes of my dad who never even knew the thing existed.

We always knew that Mum had a spiritual connection, or rather we always knew that she liked to think she had. There was certainly something in it, as she proved on many occasions, not least when she rescued my brother from an early death when everybody else, including him, thought he only had the flu. After she had insisted on an ambulance being called, we found out that in fact he had severe blood poisoning of the leg and it was racing towards his heart. Mum also – most bizarrely – 'bought' verrucas. Yes, bought! Diana Weston, my partner for twelve years, suffered from verrucas until my mother offered to buy them from her for a few pence. They quickly disappeared. No, really, they did! There she was, Ilkeston's very own mystic chiropodist.

I wasn't wholly surprised when I discovered recently that my mum comes from gypsy stock. It came to light when I was making *Who Do You Think You Are?* for the BBC. It seems that my mother's ancestors were travellers from various parts of Europe who moved into Britain through the east coast of England to join the Industrial Revolution. I feel I can relate to that traveller existence: the drifting from one thing to another; the uncertainty. Being an actor definitely has elements of that itinerant lifestyle. It seems that my sister has also inherited the gypsy gene as she has given up her mortgage for life on a canal boat.

My dad has always been a determined chap (something I've inherited), but he can also be extremely stubborn and (again like me) rather prone to extreme swings of emotion. The stubborn streak shows in his refusal to stop smoking. He smoked a pipe, then he rolled his own, then he smoked cigarettes, then he went back to the pipe, then he rolled his own again, then he went back to cigarettes. You can't deny he's versatile! He's always smoked – and still does. As I write this, he's eighty-four years of age and has been told recently by the doctors that perhaps he should stop smoking. "Now come on, I've been smoking since I was twelve, I think stopping now might kill me," he said. So there's an eighty-four-year-old rebel in there. No doctor – or government – is going to stop him from smoking.

As a child, I remember him talking at union meetings, speaking up with great conviction in support of his fellow workers. That same man, capable of such compassion, could also make apparently racist remarks. To be fair, I don't think Dad is a racist; not in the strict sense of colour prejudice anyway. Indeed, one apprentice of his, George, was among the first Jamaican immigrants to appear in Ilkeston in the Fifties. They worked together for about a year and he became very much a part of our family, bringing his 'snap' and his flask back to our house with Dad at dinnertime (lunch!). But George found life in England, particularly in the bleak East Midlands, quite severe – he must have felt very isolated in that totally white community. He tried to insist on walking in the road, not on the pavement alongside my father, but Dad would say, "We'll have none of that, get up here with me," and they did become firm friends. The truth is that Dad shares an old-fashioned image of Britain with many others of his generation; a nationalism that seems so outdated now. He fought a war for his country, lost a brother in that great conflict, and is fiercely patriotic. Norman is a good man. An honest man. But a man full of contradictions.

For all the forthright union stuff, my dad, like my mum, was fun to be with at home. They were both practical jokers, especially Mum. When we lived in my grandfather's house, my dad built himself a photographic enlarger out of a tin can, a bit of flex and a light bulb. He was very ingenious. My mother had always told us that the house was haunted by her Uncle Jack. He'd smoked a pipe and she said she always knew when he was there because she could smell the tobacco. Late one night, my father was in his little 'cupboard' (soon to become our bathroom

– yes, we still had an outside lav!), working on his photographs with the enlarger, when he suddenly smelt the dreaded tobacco. All the stories that my mother had told him started swirling through his mind, frightening the life out of him. As he pushed open the door, fearing the worst, what should he see but my mother lying on the floor, puffing on a pipe and blowing the smoke underneath the door. So… was she a spiritualist? Was she really a mystic? Possibly not. But she was certainly away with the fairies and we all loved her.

Inspired by my mother, we are a family of practical jokers and this comes out in all sorts of situations – including the night before Mum's funeral when her body came to rest in our parlour. This is a very outdated and unnecessary tradition and something I don't recommend, particularly if you have children, as it distresses everyone and probably scars them for life. Indeed all of us found it difficult for some years to picture my mother other than as she looked in the parlour that night. We had been warned by the lady from the Co-op that Mum had gone a little blue, but we went ahead anyway and the whole family gathered to pay their respects; to talk about her and leave little gifts in her coffin. The whole occasion was saved by my sister. For a while the room went very quiet and it was during the silence that my sister suddenly shouted "Boo!" – or something equally daft – at which point we all completely cracked up with laughter. My sister said it was something my mother would have done and would have enjoyed.

Mum's creative streak (perhaps mischievous is a better word than creative) soon rubbed off and I had a vivid imagination of my own from an early age. When I was very young, I built a rocket with John Windmill – a neighbour from two doors away

– that was going to take us to the moon. Actually, this rocket was a box at the bottom of the garden – hidden from sight under a privet hedge. We used to put things into it ready for the big journey, planning to leave on a particular morning at nine o'clock. It was all set between us, but the night before the launch I got very frightened. I got so worked up that I made myself ill in order not to go to the moon. When John Windmill came to the door the next day, my mum had to tell him I wasn't in. That's how my imagination was and still is – too vivid by half.

If my sister is right, and my mother was trying to contact me on that car journey, perhaps she was trying to make an apology for one particular event that happened when I was about ten years old. I haven't talked about this much – which is interesting in itself – even though I've been very aware of it being on my mind throughout my life.

My mother fell pregnant with my sister but my parents didn't tell me. I found out by reading a letter from my Aunt Elsie in London. She was my mum's sister and they used to correspond a lot. I knew it was a special letter because when they sent letters from London back then they sent them in airmail-style envelopes. I found the letter next to my mum's bed, took it into my bedroom and read it by torchlight under the bedclothes. "We're all so thrilled about the news of your new arrival," it said.

I thought, what do they mean? New arrival? Something's coming and they haven't told me. I began putting two and two together and realised the significance of a 'new arrival' coming, even though – obviously – I didn't know how it all came about.

Of course, now I know that the reason they didn't tell me was because of our circumstances at the time. Both my parents had suffered with their health. When I was very young, my dad was seriously ill with TB of the kidney, so ill in fact that he had to have a kidney removed at the age of twenty-two, a year after he came out of the Navy. It was a major operation in those days. He was given that really scary drug, streptomycin, which they hadn't properly tested at that time and which had some nasty side effects, all of which he had to cope with. Strangely, my sister and I developed a pigmentation of the skin, which a doctor in Sri Lanka diagnosed for me as a genetic disorder from Dad's use of the drug. We were told to treat the condition with a dandruff shampoo – it went away *and* we've never had dandruff! I've got pictures of how he looked back then – he was so frail. He returned to work fairly quickly after the operation but constantly had to take time off with various problems. So, throughout much of my infancy, he was very ill and couldn't work.

TB had figured prominently in Dad's family. His father, Jesse, had died of the disease in his early fifties – having survived being blown up in the trenches. Despite TB being very common in our area before, during and after the Second World War, it just wasn't talked about. Today that seems odd, but back then it was a bit like cancer was a few years ago. Now people are a bit more open about it all – any sense of stigma or shame has gone.

When I got 'pleurisy and pneumonia' my parents, naturally, fearing the dreaded TB, were terrified, and so when I finally made it out of the san I got the kid-gloves treatment for a couple of weeks. They took me to Mablethorpe for a week's holiday – just Mum, Dad and me. Because I'd been in bed for so long and was so weak I spent most of the holiday in a wheelchair, which I was really embarrassed about. Mablethorpe was where all TB patients went after the sanatorium, to the coast and the sea air.

I'm not sure whether Mum and Dad were trying to hide the

reality of TB from me or whether they didn't want to acknowledge it themselves. I'm not sure it fitted into the pattern of how they faced up to things. I just don't know. Even now it's difficult to ask Dad because he gets very defensive. He still says, "You didn't have TB!" and gets all sharp about it, and I say, "No, but I did." I think they shut it off in their heads, just got on with it and didn't dwell on things. It was their way of coping with family problems. Perhaps that's a working-class thing. You just shut a problem off, almost as if it doesn't exist.

Added to my father's kidney problems, my mother had been through two near-fatal miscarriages before I was born and, in fact, very nearly lost her life when she gave birth to me at home in my grandma's front bedroom. They had to rush in Doctor Powell, our family doctor, to deliver me after nine hours of labour. In 1949, can you imagine? He said that Mum was so lucky to survive. Upstairs my dad could hear my mum yelling (hardly surprising as I was a nine-and-a-half-pound baby!) and there he was at the bottom of the stairs, sobbing his heart out. He just said, "Never again. Never again," because he was so ill that he didn't have the strength to help her. (What man *can* help a woman at such a time? I know when my daughter was born, I hyperventilated so much that *I* was given gas and air!) On top of all that, when I was born my parents were 'brassic' and we had to live with my grandmother – they couldn't afford a place of their own.

Against this backdrop my mother fell pregnant again, as I learned from the discovered letter. Up to that point I had been on my own, an only child. The day I made the discovery about the new arrival they were knitting in front of the stove, the 'they' being my mother and my two grandmothers. It was a tiny

25

little room. It was seven in the evening. I'll never forget it. My dad was out – he was probably at a union meeting followed by a couple of pints and a game of darts with his 'brothers'– and I was waiting for Charlie Drake to come on the television. Do you remember Charlie Drake's TV shows? "Hello my darlings!" He used to do pratfalls and slapstick – I loved Charlie Drake when I was that age. It was a Tuesday night and I was desperate to see it. It started at half past seven and ran until eight o'clock – and then TV finished for the night.

Anyway, out of the blue, while I was waiting for the programme to start, my mother said: "Where's that toy your dad bought you for Christmas?"

"Which one?" I replied.

"The car that fills with petrol and goes round. Where is it? It was really expensive. What have you done with it?"

I told her it was, "Upstairs under my…"

"GO AND GET IT!" she shouted.

I did all this 'pretending-to-go-upstairs-and-look' routine, then sheepishly said: "I can't find it."

She demanded: "WHERE IS IT?"

Finally, I admitted: "I've swapped it."

"YOU'VE DONE WHAT?"

She started to look really strange and I added: "Andrew Davis – he's got it down at Larklands Avenue."

"GO AND GET IT. NOW!"

I hesitated: "It's getting dark and Charlie Drake's coming on in a minute."

But the yelling just got louder: "GO AND GET IT NOW!"

It was indeed getting dark, but I walked all the way from my estate down to Larklands Avenue – no small distance. I knocked on the front door, gripped by fear. I knew that some-thing bad was going to happen. I could sense it. Andrew Davis opened the door.

"Can I have my toy back?" I asked.

And he replied: "I've taken it apart."

"What do you mean?"

He brought this box to the door and it was all in tiny, tiny bits. The car. It was all gone.

I remember walking back home, clutching the box all the way, thinking, 'Oh my God, I want to see Charlie Drake, I want to see Charlie Drake. There's going to be trouble!'

I vividly remember delaying my entrance into the house by using privet leaves as a reed to make a trumpet sound to enter-tain myself in the street, but the only sound I could make was a raspberry and the rain hurried me into the entry. Now an 'entry', for those unacquainted with council houses in the East Midlands, was a covered alley joining the houses, usually where people kept coal but, for a child, it was usually a safe refuge from the weather and a place to play at night. But I knew it wasn't going to be a safe haven for me. Nothing was. I swallowed hard and entered the kitchen. I could hear the clicking of knitting needles and the hushed chatter in the living room. Just as I was sticking the box into the larder – well, the cupboard under the stairs – my mother confronted me: "Where is it?"

I shouted back: "It's here. It's fine. It's in the box. I've got it. Look!"

But she said: "Bring it here."

That was when it all erupted. My mother just lost it… com-pletely lost it. She started beating me with her big wooden knitting needles. I think they must have been a Size 1 – they certainly felt like it; I mean they were like proper sticks and she was really flailing away with them.

She was always prone to quite serious bursts of temper, but this was something else altogether. I was ten – about the same age as my son Sam is now. I look at Sam and think of him being thrown on the floor and beaten with two sticks! There were welts all over me. My two grandmothers were pulling her off me – pleading with her to stop; I was trying to crawl behind the sofa to get away; and, all the while, I was trying to watch Charlie Drake on TV. I always thought that I'd been really evil and deserved the beating – I mean I'd swapped a toy! Now I'm not so sure and can see the rejection from my own mother at a time when I knew I was no longer going to be the only child – very confusing for a young boy.

When I was living with Diana Weston she had a very serious miscarriage and I didn't behave at all well at that time, or at least that's what I've been told since – I suppose I wasn't aware of my own behaviour. It was almost as if I was accusing her of having had a miscarriage. She suggested I see someone because as she put it, "You've got a problem." Off I went to a Harley Street counsellor, yes – a 'shrink', a really old guy recommended by my GP. I wasn't very happy about going because I've always been very distrustful of psychiatrists.

"Do you have any problem with women?" he said. I was groaning inwardly at the predictability of it all, thinking 'this man cannot be serious', but he persisted: "I'm just trying to work out if there's any kind of event in your life… you know, if you can think of an incident that perhaps could help explain…" For some reason, out of the blue, I mentioned the knitting needle story and he said, "Oh my God! You poor boy! You swapped a toy and your mother did that to you?" And I went, "No but..." and was trying to defend my mother. Again he said, "She hit you for swapping a toy?" Sitting opposite a man charging me £120 an hour, I was trying to explain to him that, forty years previously, it was the norm for women to do this to their children. "Really?" he said. I felt myself 'going' and all I wanted to do was cry.

I think that incident with my mother affected more than just my relationship with women. In some strange way I think it also shaped the real love/hate relationship that I have with my career, with acting. I'm certainly prone to these feelings of self-doubt, to the extent that I'll sabotage what I'm doing, I'll walk away before I have the chance to mess it up – even while it might be a run-away success. I'll give it everything and then suddenly go, "Oh stuff it, I don't care." At least that way I'm in control. It's what happened on *Citizen Smith*... but more of that later.

My friend, the writer Alan Bleasdale, has a really strong belief that all of our actions are affected by incidents in our childhood. His drama *Jake's Progress* is about just that and his *GBH*, in which I also appeared, centres on a man haunted by his past. I'm inclined to agree with him – I now understand that the 'Charlie Drake incident' has affected the rest of my life. But it's taken me years to realise that: to appreciate that children can have a lasting response to particular events and that adults won't always realise the long-term repercussions of how they deal with their children. It doesn't matter what the incident is. For example, some time ago my son Jamie bit me on my leg. I was hugging him and he bit me so hard, I shouted "JAMIE!" really angrily. I shook him and he burst into tears, great globules. He looked so vulnerable and upset, so I just grabbed him and hugged him because I now know that those are moments you remember all your life.

All this stuff was going through my head as I drove to the hospital on that New Year's Eve car journey. It was like I was back in my mother's kitchen, cowering from the blows all over again. With my mother holding on in the hospital in Leicester until I got there, I think now that perhaps she was saying sorry to me. Even at the time I think she knew that she'd overdone it with the knitting needles because after that – although, of course, she raised her voice quite a few times – she never, ever, struck me again.

With incidents like that, I don't think it's just the children that are affected. It's the parents too. My mother probably frightened herself as much as she did me. More recently I've thought about it a lot from her point of view. I realise now that it was only just after the war. The effects of rationing were still being felt and we were living in a council house with tiny rooms, a small fire and a kitchen that barely had room to swing a knitting needle!

It's difficult to grasp now that Christmas in the Fifties wasn't about getting lots of presents, it was about getting just one main present – like the one that year that ended up in pieces in its box. It was a lovely red tin car, a VW probably, which had been beautifully made in Germany as all quality toys were at the time – much to my father's disgust. It came with its own petrol pump garage and a little green light even came on as it went round and round. My friends were impressed: "Wow! Fantastic! Made in Germany. Whoa!" It was *the* present. And, of course, what did I do? I swapped it.

Now I can see the desperation of Mum and Dad's situation. My father had been seriously ill and, while Mum was coping with that, she had to live with people she probably didn't want to be living with and was expecting a baby where the previous three – two of them miscarriages – had nearly killed her. She must have been in a hell of a psychological state.

The arrival of a new sister and then, later, a brother, made me an immediate 'grown-up', because I started looking after 'the kids'. With both parents working to try and keep the family, I had to lend a hand looking after Lorraine and Andrew, changing nappies and all the rest of it. It was just normal to be helping out doing that, particularly with Mum going out to work, which she had always done.

She worked variously in the Raleigh and the Players factories in Nottingham when I was a kid. I never knew what work she actually did when I was very young, but later she was a cleaner and caterer at different colleges and schools. She worked in canteens – seems a quaint old word now, doesn't it – and she was very popular. They all adored Mum.

At home, there was always a great sense of community. Our door was never locked; it was open to everyone. I don't think we ever sat down for a meal without a neighbour, friend or distant family member sitting with us. My parents were quite sociable and often went out at the weekends. They were members of the Pioneer Working Man's Club, which I hated. I spent hours in the back room drinking pop, eating crisps and playing on empty beer crates with any other kids who were around, making up silly games – the games only children can play.

Looking back, I can see I was quite a loner as a child, living a lot in my imagination. Before Lorraine and then Andrew arrived I was totally on my own, and spent most of my time living in a complete fantasy world. Sometimes, of course, I played with other children, but usually I amused myself. Play rarely involved my mum or dad, although in my dad's case that was because he was so ill. With the arrival of my siblings, of course, it all changed because suddenly there were three of us children. Perhaps that's why I'm so practical now, because I had to switch from being just me and my imagination to being quite together and responsible, looking after – or helping to look after – two kids. I suspect that's why I've always found it very difficult to let go, to have fun, as I had to grow up at a young age.

Although I doted on my younger brother, Andrew, I could be cold and very indifferent to my sister. On occasion, I treated her badly for no reason at all and, thinking back, I suspect this was the first indication of the problems I would have with women.

My first few years were spent at Grandma Stevenson's house because my parents couldn't afford a place of their own. I've got great memories of that house on Larklands Avenue with its wonderful garden that Grandma loved and a big greenhouse full of grapes. When I was five years old we went to Ashdale Road, Mum and Dad's first council house. After that we moved to 12 Inglefield Road when I was about six or seven. When you moved to a council house in the Fifties, they used to take all your furniture, put it in the removal van, lock the van and then 'gas' everything. I think it was called 'stoving'. It was done to try and combat the dual problems of infection and fleas. I can still see all the furniture just left there in the parlour when we got to the new house. For weeks we didn't have anything to use. We'd just be sitting on boxes. I said, "Why can't we have the sofa?" and my parents replied, "You can't. It's got to be in that room for three weeks." It was all sealed off. The 'gas', the stench of it, was disgusting. God knows what they actually used.

I lived mainly in council houses throughout my childhood. Years later I was able to buy my parents their own house, although it wasn't their first break from rented council property. That came not long before I left home, when I was sixteen or seventeen. The long and the short of it was that Granddad Dunmore (that's my mum's father), who was invalided out of the First World War with serious deafness, gave his house – a tiny little house – to my mum.

Granddad had the parlour, which he used as his bedsit, and we had one small room, our living room. The house also had a little kitchen, an outside toilet, a yard of a garden and three very small bedrooms upstairs. Mine was the back bedroom, which Dad also used as a dark room to develop photographs. Andrew and Lorraine were sharing the middle bedroom and then Mum and Dad were at the front of the house. Under each bed was a chamber pot, or 'jerry' as we all called it – except for Dad who referred to it as the 'pittle-pot'. Having been in the war, he refused to use the word 'jerry'! We had to use it during the night as there was only the outside toilet or 'lav'.

I didn't really get to know Granddad Dunmore because I left home soon after that move. As I discovered when I did *Who Do You Think You Are?*, he was blown up at Gallipoli in the First World War – twice within eight hours – which is why he was stone deaf. His side of the family had middle-class aspirations, but my mum's other side, the Hallsworths, had a bit of a reputation. My father was warned not to marry into the Hallsworths because they were regarded as a rough lot from an undesirable part of town. The story goes that my dad smashed the table in an argument over whether he should marry Mum. He thumped his hand hard on the table during a row with his mother and said, "I am marrying that woman, I am not marrying her family. If you try and stop me you'll say goodbye to me." And, of course, he did marry her after *that* bus ride.

My Great-Grandfather Hallsworth was a very dodgy guy. At least that's always been the impression. I don't really know any of the details about his character other than that he had fathered a lot of children. Apparently it was said that he had only to take his trousers off to make a baby – whatever that meant. Actually, if I can offer some advice here: in my experience, it is certainly easier to make babies if you do take your trousers off!

I do know that my mother's side of the family was very different from my father's. Maybe that is where I get the lighter side of my own character from as I'm pretty sure I get my darker side from my dad. Everyone on that side of the family, myself included, has this rather sombre, bleak side that appears every so often. My brother and sister have it. My dad certainly has it.

I can see it in Dad now. Sometimes it even strikes me as amusing. I can point it out to him and we can talk about it more openly, unlike years ago when you couldn't mention things like 'depression' or 'moods' or suchlike – they were just things you had to deal with, as in "Oh! Shurrup... get on with it... I'm just a bit off colour." My brother's the same: he's got everything going for him, yet sometimes when I speak to him he's *so* low, but can't explain it.

One angle on this may be that people who are not academic are more emotionally charged; they can find it difficult to express their feelings and get angry as a result. Added to which, a lack of formal academic qualifications can give people, quite wrongly, a low opinion of themselves. I can remember once bringing home a friend, Kevin Robinson, a director who I had worked with during my time at Exeter. My dad just adored him and said, "You must bring Kevin up again when you next come home."

But once I'd mentioned that Kevin had been to Oxford, that was it. My dad couldn't relate to him in the same way, but then I too was always intimidated by a superior education.

What my family suffer from could be called depression, but really it's more like a mild form of split personality, with a real happy-go-lucky element on one side and this kind of darkness on the other. I'm convinced that it's particularly common in the part of the country that I grew up in.

DH Lawrence captured the whole feeling – he came from the same area. If you look at Lawrence's work, there's this great expressive poetry to it, but then also a real darkness in some of the stories. And it's that mixture which seems so prevalent in my part of the East Midlands. It's in my work too. If you look at the stuff I've always been good at it's not overtly funny but it's not consistently bleak either – it's right in the middle. It's the guy who is entertaining but troubled. I think that's why I was drawn to the Archie Rice role in *The Entertainer*. He's a man who is up and out there and yet is haunted by his demons.

The weird thing is that while my mum's side were always frowned upon as the villains of the family, they were always so optimistic. Real Cavaliers. There was a great sense of fun in our house, despite the other, darker side. Maybe that's where the duality in *me* comes from; the two sides of the family have given me that 'split' personality and a rather flippant disregard for authority and seriousness. Perhaps that is why I have sometimes scarred my standing in the profession.

I don't think my father's parents' opposition to my mother's family was based merely on them being happy-go-lucky. Maybe in part perhaps, but there was more to it than that, something more dangerous. They viewed them as being anti-religious. My father's family were Church of England and *very* Church of England at that. High Church in fact. My grandmother used to read the Bible in bed. She also had a bowl of brazil nuts permanently by her bed to which I would help myself; at least I did until I told my father who explained to me that they were what was left of her favourite chocolate brazils after she had sucked all the chocolate off. Apparently her false teeth prevented her from chewing the nuts themselves!

I knew about her bedtime brazils and Bible reading because I used to share a bed with her in our first council house. It seems almost unbelievable now, but it wasn't uncommon then. It must have been between the ages of five and seven. My mother was dead against it and always said, "He shouldn't be sharing beds with old people." But, for reasons I didn't understand at the time, Grandma Stevenson had come to live in our house and ended up in my bed.

TWO

EARLY DRAMAS

Up to the moment I started school, my only close friend was a boy called Michael, except that he didn't really exist other than in my head. We were very close and I talked to him all the time, until one fateful day when the postman caught me talking to him. When I turned round, Michael had gone and I never saw him again.

So, when I arrived at Kensington Infant School, aged five, I was to make a real friend, a boy named Graham Sisson, who sobbed his heart out as we went through the gates. I held him all the way through the first morning, trying to comfort him as the crying continued. We ended up going all the way through our schooling together. When we'd finished our O-levels at sixteen and were leaving secondary school in the summer, going off to do whatever it was that we were going to do, he sobbed his heart out again. I can remember putting my arm around him and saying, "Don't worry, we'll keep in touch."

In the way of the world, of course, we didn't. However, many, many years later, when I was doing *Me and My Girl* at the Adelphi

Theatre in London, I received a letter from his wife saying, "Graham always talks about you, how wonderful you were as friends and how you grew up together. He'd just love to come and see the show, but we can't get tickets – is there any chance you could arrange it?" So I did. I arranged four tickets for him and his wife and two children for a Saturday night. After the show, lo and behold, he came through my dressing room door and burst into tears! All those years and I was still holding him up.

My time at that first school, Kensington, was a brilliant period for me. I was always absorbed in imaginary play, usually in a fantasy world. I silenced an art class once – I must have been six or seven – just by saying the words "Lost in space"! The entire room went from riotous noise to absolute quiet. I pitched my outburst in such a way that it was like a half whisper. I did it deliberately to see if I'd get any attention and when I got it, and saw their hushed and open-mouthed response, I said to myself, 'I did that.'

A rather unusual achievement perhaps, but the fact that I could do that, that I could grab the attention of the whole class, left a lasting impression on me. Later on, Mr Wearmouth, my English teacher, was the one who made me read out loud. I was chosen to tell the Friday afternoon story on more than one occasion. I read from *The Wind in the Willows* and I loved it, just loved it. So my passion for reading – and especially for reading out loud – had begun.

At the end of my time at Kensington my life took an abrupt – and for me, shocking – turn. Indeed today, more than four decades on, it still holds a prominent place in my psyche. I was in the 'A' class and was expected to pass my eleven-plus, but I failed. Miserably. It was such a surprise, and not just for me and my parents – Mr Wearmouth and the headmaster seemed as shocked as we were. My dad still has a letter from one of them saying, "We cannot understand…" and so on. As a result, or rather as a lack of a result, I was to go to the local secondary modern, Gladstone Boys', a school that had a fierce and terrible – and I mean really terrible – reputation.

There was no uniform at Gladstone Boys', although there seemed to be an unofficial dress code of leather jacket and bike chain. The place had such a rough, awful image. *And* it was a single sex school. Boys only. Which was a shame, because I was just beginning to get the idea of girls towards the end of my time at Kensington. But then I was off to Gladstone Boys'.

Everyone knew and dreaded what happened to all the new boys who entered Gladstone. As part of your initiation you were put inside a dustbin. It was then shut, chained up and thrown down the school steps (Lord knows what they do today, in the era of wheelie bins…).

That's what happened in most cases and so I got ready to face the ordeal. But somehow, someway, I bluffed my way out of it. There I was, due to go the quick way down those school steps and very scared about the prospect – I mean, there had been some serious accidents – and yet I got out of it. I don't know how I did it, but I did. Maybe I made the lads laugh or perhaps I used that old trick from the Westerns: if you pretended to be insane, the Indians would leave you alone! Suddenly it was all over and the bell went and that was it.

Going to Gladstone Boys' was a shock to the system in many ways. It was a disappointment to me, to my teachers and to my parents. There were several of us who were expected to pass

the eleven-plus but who failed, and it caused a lot of contro-
versy. Graham Sisson, who went from Kensington to Gladstone
with me, was a good student, very bright mathematically, so
there was no reason why he should have failed the exam. And
I was supposedly great at English, so we couldn't really understand why I hadn't made the grade either. My parents went to
the school and had a moan, as did a lot of others. I've since
been told that the exam changed to more of a multiple-choice
format around that time, and that perhaps the results were
skewed because some schools were slow in grooming children
for the new-style exam. But who knows? I don't know now
and I didn't know then – and neither, seemingly, did my teachers.

Later, when I was thirteen, I got this chance, this opportunity, to go to Nottingham High School, a very famous grammar
school where DH Lawrence was taught, but my parents couldn't
afford it. That broke my mother's heart, it really did, because
her and Dad had such aspirations for me to have an academic
life. They didn't show any disappointment at the time, however, and were very supportive, as they always had been.

It was a big thing to pass the eleven-plus. So big that a lot
of children were promised things like a new bike if they passed.
For me, there was nothing like that. Bribes or blackmail weren't
part of my life, simply because my parents couldn't afford it.
As I've already mentioned, my Christmas was always limited
to one major present. Perhaps I'd also get a *Beano* annual, maybe
some fruit or nuts and a present from an aunt. That's all. I find
the current concept of Christmas and kids shocking, with the
sheer number of presents they get. For me, as for most kids
growing up in the Fifties, the fun of Christmas came from games
and activities rather than gifts. My memories are of Christmas

family get-togethers where each person would get up and do something: it could be a song, a magic trick or it could simply be falling over. It was pure entertainment. Just get up and do something even if it was, come to think of it, usually just falling over, simply!

We played fantastic, fun games like Kissing the Blarney Stone. You were made to wear a blindfold and to kiss what would turn out to be the bend of your father's arm. As you took your blind-fold off, he'd be pulling up his trousers to make you think that you had kissed your own father's arse! Well, it seemed funny at the time but I won't be playing it with my kids! That was part of the tradition growing up in my house – Mum and Dad both loved to 'perform'. But those traditions seem to have disappeared from the modern Christmas. Today, it seems like we're all too busy to do anything like that, with far too many distractions from simple fun.

Anyway, incentive or no, I failed the eleven-plus and Glad-stone Boys' it was. I suppose it seems churlish now to moan about failing the exam, about being 'a failure' – you might say it hasn't held me back – but back then, coming from the back-ground that I did, it meant everything. Now of course I can't see my life in any other way. It certainly shaped me and I would be very different had I not gone there.

Although I'm not exactly proud of my school, of Gladstone Boys', I'm certainly not ashamed of it. The only time I've economised with the truth about my secondary modern educa-tion was when Tom Courtenay proposed me for membership of The Garrick Club. He rang me and said, "The application form asks about your education. What shall I put?" I proudly said, "Gladstone Secondary Modern Boys' School," to which he responded, "Gladstone *Secondary Modern* Boys' School," emphasising the secondary modern bit, "I can't put that. Not for the Garrick. I'll just put Gladstone Boys' and RADA."

One of the first teachers, or masters as we had to call them, that I met at Gladstone Boys' was Mr Thompson, known as 'Big Tom'. We had a 'Little Tom' who taught English and music in Room Ten and, opposite him across the hall, 'Big Tom' taught in this very Victorian classroom. You had to go up some steps to get to it. It had the old inkwells in the desks and a big blackboard complete with shutters. Out of a back room, after we'd entered for our first class, came 'Big Tom'. The vision was striking. He was a hunchback and really did look like Charles Laughton in *The Hunchback of Notre Dame* (or he did to us kids at least). He stared us down, defying anyone to laugh, assessing our reactions. We all sat there aghast. He really was the most extraordinary-looking individual. Looking back now it seems a real shame that I never got to know him – apparently he was a wonderful artist as well as being a master at the school. Poor old 'Big Tom'. Wonderful 'Big Tom'.

The most important teacher for me at Gladstone Boys', and someone who was to recognise my ability, was this great man called John Lally. When I got there he was the art master and was installed in a little wooden hut, a temporary classroom, at the side of the main school playground. John was an amazing character; a huge, eccentric bear of a man who wore tweeds and brogues and waistcoats and fob chains and was always immaculately dressed. He had a booming voice and was very, very eloquent. Everyone loved him. At speech days he'd just give the best oration about the year's events.

He was the one that got me involved in acting and performing.

Only *he* could have formed a drama group called The Grand Order of Thespians at a rough, tough, secondary modern school. It was brilliant because it united the school. Everyone got involved in the school play: he got the maths department doing the box office, the metalwork department doing the set, and the technical drawing department doing the designs. Everyone was involved in some way or another.

He made me 'Grand Thespian' and it was thrilling and inspiring. We had meetings on a Tuesday night in the Art Room and we'd be there in robes, with me sitting on a throne. There was always a real buzz to it. For us, it was a major event in the week, a time when we discussed plays and what we were going to do on stage. Before you knew it, everyone was caught up in the atmosphere – it produced this really exciting sense of importance.

We did several school plays, all of which were in the school hall on a terrible, tiny little stage. I haven't been able to go back and see it all, the 'scene of the scenes' as it were, because they've demolished the school and built a ring road through it. I thought ring roads were meant to go round towns; that one went right through the middle of town, and right through Gladstone Secondary Modern Boys' School. There was a huge outcry when they knocked the old school down because it was a listed building and, more importantly, DH Lawrence actually taught there for a spell in Room One.

John Lally got me involved in drama and even persuaded me to join in with local amateur dramatic groups, not something I was initially a great fan of as some of the people were rather eccentric and they all seemed a bit remote from anything that I knew and understood. I couldn't see amateur dramatics as a way of life for me at that time and the school's Grand Order of Thespians was so much more 'me'.

When I went to The Ilkeston Theatre Club for the first time, I got as far as the door. I thought, 'I can't go in there.' I left and ended up going to see some Elvis movie at the cinema. Eventually I did make it over the threshold – the theatre club had heard some good things about me from the teachers at school, so they came down to find me and I joined up.

My enjoyment of drama convinced me to go for a place at Clarendon College, the only college in the area with a drama programme attached to the A-level courses. John Lally helped prepare me for the audition. On one occasion we were on the school assembly stage during lesson time, so it was all quiet in the hall, and he was taking me through *Henry V*:

"Once more unto the breach, dear friends, once more;
Or close the wall up with our English dead..."

He was explaining the gravity of the speech to me; that you're motivating people going forward into battle and so on and so forth. About halfway through the speech, the school bell rang and all the lads came out from the classrooms. John Lally shouted "Quiet!" and made everybody, every one of 480 boys, listen to me.

Inwardly I was screaming 'My God!' All my enemies, all my mates, all lined up, standing there, staring at me, with their leather jackets on, collars turned up, all dying to go to the toilets or to have a fag behind the bike sheds. It was a terrifying sight. "Don't make me do it!" I groaned, but I knew I had no choice – I had to let go and soldier on:

"But when the blast of war blows in our ears,
Then imitate the action of the tiger:
Stiffen the sinews, conjure up the blood,
Disguise fair nature with hard-favoured rage..."

Eventually, warming to the role, I got into the rally at the end:

"I see you stand like greyhounds in the slips,
Straining upon the start. The game's afoot:
Follow your spirit; and upon this charge
Cry, 'God for Harry, England and Saint George!'"

A brief pause, and then the place erupted in cheering. "Yeah!!!" It was quite fantastic. It gives me a small thrill even now, thinking about it, writing about it. It was like, 'Whoa!' John beamed at me and said "See!" I remember him just standing there as they cheered. I was up and running. I remember that day as a real turning point; I remember thinking, 'I want to do more of this.' It gave me confidence in *me* for the first time – or rather the 'me' that I wanted to be.

It also helped me face some of the more physical challenges of Gladstone. There were some real fights at school. John Lally made me a prefect, which meant that I was always seen as being on the 'them' side, as it were. The 'us' side were the rebels – and there were some real James Dean-type guys at that school. I'd been bullied by two of them. They were really dangerous, from a bad part of town (probably my mum's!). One of them challenged me to a fight, which was going to take place on the last day of school – the day I was due to leave for good – outside the school gates. Walking along with Graham Sisson, I got out onto the school steps and I could hear my surname being chanted: "Stevo... Stevo." I walked up and out through the gates and the entire school were waiting at the end of Extension Street, standing in a big crowd, braying. It was like a cauldron. I knew I had to go into that ring, and genuinely thought I was going to get a really good hiding. My opponent was standing there waiting, hitting the palm of one hand with the fist of the other (he'd clearly been watching the right films). I thought, 'I can't get out of this one, I can't get out of this like I got out of the dustbin one.'

In my head was a story that my dad had told me about when he was a young lad and was challenged to a fight on a canal bank by some roughneck. My dad said that as the lad went to take his jacket off – in the time-honoured tradition of small town dust-ups – he hit him really hard while his arms were still trapped in his jacket. That had stuck in my mind. It came back to me then at my *High Noon* moment. I remember walking towards him. He had his leather jacket on and he said, "Right Stevo," and started to take it off. I knew this was my moment and I whacked him so hard that it felt like my knuckles went back up into my arm. He went down... and he stayed down. I remember standing there saying, "I've killed him, I've killed him." And there was Graham, sobbing his heart out. The next thing I knew the lads were chanting, "Yeah... Stevo... Stevo." Suddenly, I was the 'cock' of the school.

That was my last day of school, aged sixteen. It was 1966 – the World Cup year, of course – and that's when, during the summer, I went to London to stay with my aunt and uncle down in Edmonton. It was my first taste of London, a brief introduction before I returned home and enrolled at Clarendon College.

As a summer treat, my aunt and uncle took me and my cousin Barbara to the coast. We were on Southend beach I remember – gawd help us, on Southend beach of all places – when England won the World Cup. Even though we were on the beach there were televisions everywhere, all wired up from the bars and clubs on the front. But these were old tellies, not like the plasma monsters of today, and they wheeled the tiny screens outside. Even now it's hard to imagine the event actually taking place 'in colour'!

THREE

LOSING MY VOICE

So, in September 1966 I went to Clarendon College in Nottingham to study drama for two years. But at first all I studied were the girls. Well, I had just spent five years at a boys' school!

I could go on about all the affairs I had with the hairdressing students at Clarendon (but I won't!). They were there because it was a College of Further Education – it certainly furthered my education. I was there because it also ran a drama course. I recall a certain squash court that saw a lot of action, none of it involving the game of squash! Clarendon was my sexual awakening – well it would be wouldn't it? It was when I got to know a bit about life.

I was surrounded by beautiful girls – Clarendon and Nottingham were known for them – and it seemed that the college was just full of women. There were hundreds, literally hundreds of them from the secretarial course, the hairdressing course and the drama course among others. Nottingham has two lions in Slab Square that I should mention. Legend has it that the lions get up and roar whenever a virgin passes by. Nobody has ever seen them move. I'll let you draw your own conclusions about whether that proves or disproves the legend!

Clarendon was bliss. I had such a good time. At the start I lived at home in Ilkeston and travelled daily into college and back, even though it was quite a journey. I don't think I ever took the bus all the way in either direction, because I couldn't afford the full bus fare. I'd get a bus from Ilkeston to Nottingham, pay for that part of the journey and then have to walk from Nottingham to Clarendon, which was about five and a half miles from the city centre. Unfortunately there was no family car to borrow as cars were a luxury rather than a necessity for most people back then. I can still remember the day they opened the M1 – we walked miles across the fields to Trowell in Nottinghamshire just to see it. I remember marvelling, 'That goes all the way to London.' It was empty – there was nothing on it – but it was an open road that I knew I wanted to take.

My life took on a whole new dimension at Clarendon. It was much more grown up. I even had a flat at one point – not mine, you understand, but one I was sharing when I was at the college. All of a sudden I was standing on my own two feet; living away from home and my family and working at both the Nottingham Playhouse and the local coffee bar. My job as an assistant stage manager at Nottingham Playhouse was during the period when the great John Neville was the artistic director. It was the place to be then, the *in* place, as was Nottingham itself.

I was at the college doing a combination of A-levels and O-levels. I only succeeded in getting one A-level – partly because I was too busy with the girls – but got the two more O-levels that I needed. I say 'needed' because my time at Clarendon was all geared around me getting the right qualifications to go on to drama school, not to act but to train as a drama teacher. That was the plan, always the plan – to teach – but I got mixed up with a group of guys who were all saying to me, "You should go to RADA, you wanna act."

To begin with, my parents didn't know I was going in for acting; they certainly didn't know that I was applying for RADA. Nobody did. I don't think my parents would have wanted me to do it. I don't think they really understood it at all. They would have preferred me to go for something safer than acting. They knew I was hooked on drama, but they assumed I would teach it. That I could be a teacher! That was the logical progression, I guess, and the way they – and I – thought it would unfold. But I got caught up in the world of the Clarendon glitterati of the mid 1960s – actors such as Richard Beckinsale, Ken Aitchinson, David Dixon, Granville Saxton and Richard Latham. They were all really good and all well ahead of me, not only on the acting front but also in 'living the life'. Richard Beckinsale was already married to a girl from the hairdressing course at Clarendon, had a daughter (Samantha, who I worked with on *Jake's Progress* many years later), and was living in his own flat. He was only a couple of years older than I was but it all seemed very grown up to me – being married with a child. There they were, travelling down to London… in a car, their own car… whoa! So I knew I had to catch up. And that meant breaking a few rules.

I didn't actually meet Richard Beckinsale at Clarendon – he was slightly before my time – but I always felt I knew him (as, I'm sure, did most people – that was part of his charm). I felt like I was walking in his footsteps. He was from my neck of the woods, he'd failed his eleven-plus and then ended up at Clarendon College. I followed him to RADA and into sitcoms. Later, I worked with him a couple of times and was struck by his film-star good looks and by how easy he made acting seem. He was very much a hero to me and, when he died, I was absolutely dev-astated. We were filming *Citizen Smith,* the tank episode, when word got round that he had died the previous night, aged just thirty-two.

He died of a heart attack and must have been under a lot of stress as he never, ever stopped working. When he was doing *Rising Damp* and *Porridge* back to back, he was also doing *Funny Peculiar* at the Garrick in the West End, and then went straight on to a musical. He was playing charity football on a Sunday and smoking cigars. The way he went always makes me think about the pressure that this profession can put you under. You feel like you have to do everything at once, in case the work suddenly dries up.

At some point I had to break it to my parents that I wanted to be an actor. It was easier to explain to my mother than it was to my father. At that time, he had aspirations for me to be a footballer. I was, in fact, a half-decent footballer – at least I could have made it at county level – but my heart wasn't really in it. When I announced to my dad that I wanted to become an actor and to train at the Royal Academy of Dramatic Art, he just looked at me and said, "Why don't you go right over the top and become a bloody hairdresser!"

However, of course, when I did get into RADA, for me and everyone else it was 'mega'. It made the front page of the *Ilke-ston Advertiser*. I think my dad's still got the cutting; you can guess, there's a big picture of me on the front with the caption "Royal Academy accepts local boy".

When the acceptance note arrived from RADA (my mother

always insisted on the full 'Royal Academy of Dramatic Art' – for her the 'Royal' was the most important element), my mother grabbed me and ran through Ilkeston, tapping on ground floor windows, shouting at upstairs windows and knocking on doors: "He's got in! He's got in! He's going to the Royal Academy!"

What with her and the newspaper, it went round the town like wildfire. You have to understand that if you put the word 'royal' in front of something in a place like Ilkeston at that time, you were guaranteed that people would want to know about it. It was a big achievement in our family: my mother hadn't been to college and my father had been an apprentice. They had both left school when they were only thirteen or fourteen years old.

A big achievement, except that it wasn't. At least it wasn't as far as the drama teachers at Clarendon were concerned. To them it was a failure. You see they had set me the aim of getting the two A-levels and two O-levels needed to go to the Rose Bruford drama school on a teaching course. In their eyes, that was what I was meant to be doing.

At that time you weren't really encouraged to become an actor or to go into the theatre, particularly where I came from – that was no profession for a grown man. I realise now that it was something that I must have really, really wanted to do, which in itself was quite unusual for me. I was definitely hooked on acting. There was no way I could have made it in the business if I hadn't had tunnel vision in my ambition to act. I can't put that determination solely down to the *Henry V* speech in front of the school or other, earlier incidents. I think my resolve to be an actor emerged in a whole chain of events then and later on.

I was certainly encouraged by the way I was treated at Clarendon and the way I managed to land lead roles in the productions there, notably in *A Hatful of Rain* when I played a Gladstone Boys'-type thug. That was a major event for me – the play received coverage in the Nottingham press and I even won a medal for it. I also used to win medals at various drama festivals and, like my classmates, was sent off around the country, sitting exams that were attached to the diplomas (from LAMDA and the Guildhall) that we took at Clarendon. All of these factors came together, creating a definite sequence of events through school and beyond, which made me decide to be an actor rather than a drama teacher.

It was around the time that I was leaving Clarendon, I can now see, that I began to 'get my voice', a process that would eventually strip away my native accent. It wasn't just the way I sounded, it was also the words and expressions I used like 'corsey' for pavement, 'mardy' for sulking, 'that'll learn ya' for that'll teach you and 'that's worrased' for that's what I said.

They had a tutor at the college called John Wills who tried to change the way I spoke. He was a brilliant, brilliant speaker and very camp. He used to get me to read a poem by DH Lawrence called *Giorno dei Morti* – Day of the Dead.

I was around seventeen years old when John Wills started teaching me 'RP'. This is the way he always referred to Received Pronunciation. It's meant to be the way that a reasonably educated person in London or the South East would speak; they also used to call it BBC English. Anyway, as I said, he was definitely in the Quentin Crisp mould. He used to sit with his legs *very* crossed, leaning forward with a cigarette permanently on the go. He'd sit in the middle of the hall while I would get up on stage and, in my very strong Midlands accent, start to recite *Giorno dei Morti*:

"Halongg…g the avenew of Soypresses
Alllllll in their scarrlet cloaks and surrrrrrplices
Of linen, go the…"

"No… darhling… nooo! Not 'Halonggg…g' – it's a neutral vowel sound. 'Along' – let the 'g' disappear into the nasal cavities."
"Alongg…"
"It's *Along* the avenue of cypresses…"
"Alongg…"
"Nearly – now do it again, let go and let it be you."
"Alongg…"
"No, not like that!"
"But that is me. Alonngg…"
So, I'd go home at night to Mum and Dad and say, "Halongg the avenue…" and Dad would be going, "He's doing well. He's doing well. Int'it good? I'll tell you what. If it all goes wrong and you end up a dustbin man, you'll be the best speaking one they've ever had."

By the time I went down to RADA, as you can probably imagine, vocally I was completely lost – I didn't know which way was up, how I should be talking, what the correct pronunciation was, which voice I should be using. I began to wonder who I was and who I was becoming.

The transition in my speech that began at Clarendon really gathered pace at RADA when Pamela Barnard and Michael McCallion got hold of me. They used to put this machine around my head. It was like a little headset that enabled you to hear yourself speaking. You had cups over your head and on your ears and you could hear this little voice, your own 'little voice'. Pamela and Michael would say, "Listen to yourself." I'd be thinking, 'Bloody hell!'

"That's you right now. What we want you to do is... talk like this."

And suddenly I was speaking 'like this'. Of course, when I went home at weekends, back up to Ilkeston, and saw all my old mates in The Three Horseshoes and began talking 'like this', they'd be sat there saying, "Fookin'ell Stevo! Fookin'ell!" in our normal strong 'Ilson' accent. I'd send them away in droves and end up standing there on my own. And, of course, I was in total isolation at RADA too, because there they'd be saying, "I'm sorry! What did you say?" when I spoke to them either in my native Midlands accent or my new mangled RP.

I really didn't know where I was in terms of the way I spoke so, gradually, I started being all 'London'. And I think that's why I ended up playing characters like Wolfie Smith when I got my first jobs in television.

At RADA they also taught you the Alexander Technique. I'd be walking around just as I had done at home, slightly slouchy, leading with the head in a really excited and enthusiastic way. Mrs Woodman would say, "No, no, dear boy! Put your chin in. Put your head up." They were really urging me to let go of my old ways of walking and talking. We used to have these special exercises, so we'd be walking round like that in a vertical, stiff way and talking 'like this' in a really posh voice. It was supposed to be natural!

It was a big transition for a seventeen-year-old, East Midlands, council estate, secondary-modern schoolboy. I wasn't entirely on my own in this respect of course. A lot of people made the same journey as I did.

When John Wills died I read the poem that he'd made me

work on, the *Giorno dei Morti*, at his memorial service. I did it for *him* and what it had meant to me. It's a very maudlin poem which perfectly fitted the occasion.

It's about the loss of a child. Hardly the chirpiest thing to read out, but I did it for John because he taught me so much and because we had been through that poem together with a fine-tooth comb. That's why I remember it vividly. I remember all the diphthongs and tripthongs and neutral vowels – I mean, can you imagine being taught what a neutral vowel was at seventeen years of age, having spoken with a broad accent for so long?

At John's memorial I did the poem both ways, the 'before' and the 'after', explaining how significant it had been to my life. First I did a bit of it 'my' way to lighten it all up, the way that I used to when I first went to John. It was actually quite difficult for me by then to recreate the original voice that I had and which he had first heard. Doing it that way raised a smile on a sad day, but then, because I owed it to him and as a tribute, I did the full poem just as he had wanted me to:

Giorno dei Morti

Along the avenue of cypresses,
All in their scarlet cloaks and surplices
Of linen, go the chanting choristers,
The priests in gold and black, the villagers...
And all along the path to the cemetery
The round dark heads of men crowd silently,
And black-scarved faces of womenfolk, wistfully
Watch at the banner of death, and the mystery.

And at the foot of a grave a father stands
With sunken head, and forgotten, folded hands;
And at the foot of a grave a mother kneels
With pale shut face, nor either hears nor feels

The coming of the chanting choristers
Between the avenue of cypresses,
The silence of the many villagers,
The candle-flames beside the surplices.

Thank you John. If I hadn't been able to lose my heavy accent
I would have ended up having to play DH Lawrence characters
all my life.

FOUR

SEX, DRUGS AND KEBABS

EVERYONE AT Clarendon was pretending they were going to be a teacher, feigning interest in the teacher training courses at Rose Bruford drama school in Kent, the Royal College of Music and Drama in Cardiff or the Guildhall School in London, and then going behind the tutors' backs and sneaking off to auditions for acting courses at places like RADA or Central. I had to borrow a fiver – no small sum back in 1968 – from my best friend Clare Monk for my train fare and my audition entrance fee. I made the trip down to London for the first of two auditions.

I went to stay in Edmonton with Aunt Elsie and Uncle Harry. From there I travelled all the way to Russell Square on the bus and the tube, which was a bit of a nightmare journey, and did my first audition for RADA.

No one helped with my first audition piece for RADA because I didn't even tell my tutors I was going up for it. Instead, I used to rehearse any audition routine with other actors, friends like Alan Morris, who were trying to go the same route as I was but weren't getting past the audition stage.

I got a re-call, which caused a lot of excitement, and had to go to RADA itself for the second audition. I went to the little theatre, the George Bernard Shaw Theatre, which was in the basement. I performed an extract from *Blues for Mr Charlie*, playing a black character with a bluesy Deep South accent. I can't believe I did it. In fact, I can remember the audition panel doing a collective look of "What?" The whole piece was done in this southern black drawl. It was 'Mississippi' black. Here was a patently white lad from the East Midlands auditioning, bizarrely, with the role of a black American. Well, Olivier had just played Othello – something that wouldn't happen today – and he was a big influence on young actors at the time.

It was about a guy saying how much he hated the whites because of slavery. I launched into it, jumping onto a box for dramatic effect I seem to remember. The panel included Judith Gick (who turned out to be my private tutor in the end) and a fabulous actress, Rachel Gurney (who played the very beautiful, aristocratic mother on TV in *Upstairs, Downstairs*). Anyway, I launched into this speech from *Blues for Mr Charlie* and all I remember thinking was, 'It's that woman off the telly.' Then I did a bit from *The Two Gentlemen of Verona*. It was Launce, the man with the dog – who's not funny. It's supposed to be a funny speech, but it's not, and I'm *still* thinking, 'It's that woman off the telly.' There is this problem with Shakespeare: speeches meant to be funny are notoriously difficult to do. You are told that it's funny, that it'll kill 'em in performance. Believe me, I've tried with Feste, Fabian, Launce and others. You are told by everyone that a character or speech is funny and you, wanting to believe them, go on stage like a lamb to the slaughter. One actor even said that the only reason he got a laugh with the

"Budge... budge not" Launcelot Gobbo monologue in *The Merchant of Venice* was because he'd got ginger hair.

Around the time that I was auditioning for RADA in 1968, there were probably about two to three thousand others auditioning for twenty-five places, so I knew the chances of success were slim.

After I'd done my second audition, I caught the train back to Nottingham and met all my mates. I went from the station and joined them all for a drink. They were saying "Wow, wow..." and were really excited that I'd gone to RADA and met these people (including one off the telly!). We ended up having an impromptu party in the Wine Vaults in Nottingham and my dad and mum came down and joined us. There were two guys near us who were swearing a lot, although not particularly at us. They were "fookin' this" and "fookin' that". Dad leaned over to one of them and said, "I'm terribly sorry. Would you mind keeping your voices down. I have my wife with me." The guy threatened to go and get some mates to sort us out but my dad just said, "Hurry up then, 'cos we've got a bus to catch." I couldn't believe him, but from the look in his eyes I just knew he was waiting for the bloke to take off his jacket!

My parents came round to the idea of me going to RADA, particularly when I got the re-call for a second audition. By that stage they were as excited as I was; in part, I guess, because it was actually RADA, it was big time. That would have been December/January time and I must have heard the good news about February/March – at least a two-month wait. Then, of course, we got the letter, which offered me a place on the Acting Course, provided I could confirm that I had a grant from my local authority. In those bad old good old days the local authority funded you. I was being offered a place at RADA, starting in the September of 1968, and was even given a rare scholarship, one of only about three awarded, to help a bit financially. However, my mum and I had to go to Matlock, to the head office of the local education authority, to try and secure my grant.

There was a panel of people assembled to assess my grant application. I walked into the room and they said, "What do you do? Would you mind doing it for us?" "For what reason?" I asked. "To enable us to determine whether you can have your grant," they replied. "But I've already been accepted by the Royal Academy of Dramatic Art. I've passed *their* audition," I snapped.

I had this stand-up argument with them and Mum was squirming. They were all stuffy education authority types and I got really, really angry with the fact that they were saying, in effect, that they were above the people who had auditioned me for RADA. At one point I was going to walk out. Eventually I was persuaded to back down by this English teacher on the panel – I don't know who he was. He suggested that it was probably in my best interests to actually do exactly what they were asking. So I did. Of course I did, I needed the money.

The long and short of it was that I was offered £115 per term – and that amount was meant to keep me for twelve weeks. The fees were also paid in part by the local authority, and my scholarship probably funded the rest.

Out of the £115, I think I budgeted that I would have about a fiver a week to spend – after I'd paid the rent – for food and everything else I needed. Three of us eventually rented a place together, but at first I stayed with my aunt and uncle in Edmonton. This became a nightmare when they moved up to Enfield and I had to commute from there into central London. It got really tricky: I'd be coming back at ten o'clock at night and they'd leave food in the oven for me. It would have gone all dry and crisp waiting for me – inedible in fact. I wasn't eating a lot, that's for sure.

I didn't want to upset them by leaving and I knew that my Uncle Harry really liked my company. He loved me being there because they didn't have kids and I think he always looked at me as a kind of son figure. But I was eighteen – I wanted to be free. I wanted to be independent.

So eventually, after the first term, I found myself a flat with Harry Burgess Wall and Sean Seymour. It was in King's Cross, above a fish shop and below a prostitute. Above her, lived two girls who were very high up in the Salvation Army – talk about worlds colliding! Fish shop, prostitute, three actors and two Sally Army officers. Got to be a sitcom in there somewhere... watch this space!

Once we were settled in the flat, I began knuckling down to life at RADA. Even then I was being chosen to play small parts in final-year productions, which was virtually unheard of for a first-year student. I was getting singled out by people like Gilbert Vernon, who still writes to me now. He put me in a production called *The Old Bachelor*, a Restoration comedy, and I remember I had all of four lines in it, but they got laughs and people were asking, "Blimey! Who's he? He's funny but you can't understand a word he's saying!"

We used to do improvisation at RADA. There was a company there called Theatre Machine who specialised in it. In one exercise, you pretended that you were sitting on a park bench, that you'd left RADA and it was years later – when you were much older. While you were sitting there, you'd meet someone from RADA who you hadn't seen for thirty years and the conversation would go, "Oh my God, Harry, how are you?" "Robert, haven't seen you for years, what have you been up to?" Then you would get into a whole imaginary discussion about what you'd done and achieved in the interim, or not as the case may be.

It must have been twenty years after I'd left RADA that I bumped into one of my contemporaries and it was just like doing that improv again. Or at least it should have been. In reality we hardly spoke because we just couldn't think of what to say to each other. We couldn't even improvise something.

I haven't done much improvisation in my career; to be honest it's always frightened me. I don't like that sense of being myself, of being 'exposed', and not knowing what's going to happen next. I was always good at mime, which can help, but I'm wary of on-the-spot improvisation. I had a go at improv for a TV thing once and it only served to confirm all my fears. It was a pilot for a show, filmed in front of a studio audience, and I was asked to do this improvised scene with an actress. All I was told beforehand was that I was to be an international chess player, while the actress playing opposite me belonged to the 'oldest profession in the world' – that was how they phrased it. At the time, being a rather green young man, I didn't actually know what the 'oldest profession in the world' was. Everyone else in the building – all six hundred members of the audience and the entire cast – seemed to know, but I didn't!

I figured she could have been a milkmaid or something. Eventually the audience seemed to twig that I didn't have a clue what she was. She starts coming on to me, the nerdy chess player, and the audience begins screaming with laughter. I felt incredibly embarrassed. I remember thinking, 'Oh f***, they're all laughing at me.' But they weren't. They were laughing because they thought I was doing it deliberately – that I was feigning not knowing – thinking that a chess player, in fact, *would* be the person least likely to know what the oldest profession in the world was. I was trying to come up with the kind of stuff I thought a chess grand-master might say, such as, "So it's your move now," and she'd be pulling up her skirt... more laughter!

My improvisation gaffe turned out to be a stroke of genius, but to anyone who might have been there that night I confess – I had no idea she was playing a hooker. And therein lies my problem with improvisation – I need to prepare and to get to know the character to feel confident with what I'm doing.

For my final two terms at RADA, I ended up living with a girl in a flat on Goodge Street. For both of us, it was a move born out of pure survival as much as anything, as we were broke most of the time and had absolutely nothing to live on.

I would try and work a bit during the summer to earn some much-needed money; in particular I remember selling programmes and working as an usher for the Danny La Rue show at the Palace Theatre in Shaftesbury Avenue. Roy Hudd was there too, playing Max Miller in what was a big Variety show. I got com-pletely hooked and watched every night from start to finish – I loved it! I thought Danny La Rue was brilliant and Roy Hudd was just a genius. I remember a lot of the routines, and some of the songs still stick in my mind:

'Falling in love again
What am I to do?
Although I'm seventy-two,
I can't help it.
Lifting my face again
Pulling up my skin
This is not my chin,
It's my kneecap.'

These spells of employment were during the holidays rather than term time when evenings and weekends were taken up with RADA work. Even during the holidays, I sometimes had to do preparation work for productions I was either appearing in or directing.

Funding myself at RADA wasn't easy. We all used to share with each other and sponge off anyone we could – most of us were in the same boat, I suppose. The flat I shared at the end was disgusting. It was a one-bedroom – almost a one-room – garret. It really stank, because it was above a kebab shop – Gigs Kebab House in Goodge Street. It's still there!

My first flat had been above a fish and chip shop and the last was above that kebab shop. Maybe the smell of kebabs was a slight improvement on the smell of fish. Ugh – the smell of fish and chips and the lingering odour of the boiling oil and its greasy vapours. It certainly stayed with you – on your clothes and on your mind. Funnily enough, many years later there was a line in *Me and My Girl* which really struck a chord with me: "We'll get the smell of fish off you some'ow!"

I suppose I shouldn't moan about the kebab shop too much – the guy running Gigs used to give us free meals. It was a lifeline, especially when we ran out of money at the end of the month and got really desperate; desperate enough even to 'nick' (or 'liberate' as we said in the supposedly revolutionary Sixties) the few essential items that we needed from bookshops, clothes boutiques or food stores. Financially, it was a real struggle, living hand-to-mouth all of the time and battling to find money for the course books we needed as well as everything else.

It was a bit easier for the handful of more privileged students at RADA. On the day I arrived at RADA, I was accompanied by my aunt from Edmonton. She came all the way in on the bus with me, and then got back on board and went all the way home. I resisted it but I think my mum must have asked her to take me, *still* not letting go. I was eighteen. Give me a break! As we got there, in stark contrast to my own arrival, a beautiful powder-blue Bentley or Corniche or whatever pulled up and this stunning model got out with her bags. She did that thing of touching her hair with her hand as she walked up the steps of RADA and I went "Wow!" She was gorgeous. A new student like – or rather not like – me. With a very posh voice, she said, "Oh, hello. Could you tell me where the principal's office is?" I could almost hear myself say "Halongg the avenue of cypresses…" But, we became really good friends despite the obvious difference in backgrounds.

Although essentially we were all students, there was that kind of divide between those worth a mint and those that were skint. Even so, the wealthier ones helped the rest of us out financially if we were in a fix.

Among the 'minted' at RADA there was a well-heeled American who got married to a girl I adored at the time, Patricia Martin; I liked to think she only married him to help keep him in the country because of the immigration issues. They had this absolutely crazy wedding that we all went to. Most of the guests were on marijuana. There they were, all smoking at this civil ceremony in London, all in fits of giggles. In fact, the registrar at one point insisted that the service be taken seriously.

Smoking dope and experimenting with other drugs – including LSD – was very prevalent when I was at RADA. A lot of people were into it all big-time. I was on the fringes of that scene, and always a bit on the fence when it came to the drug culture.

Obviously, I dabbled. I remember going to a *Sergeant Pepper* party where me and a pal had one puff on a joint and thought we were stoned! We were going, "Wow! Isn't it great, man?" It was four o' clock in the morning and we were walking through King's Cross, a couple of posers, acting more stoned than we can possibly have been. Most of the time I managed to concentrate on acting and absolutely nothing, or rather no one, was going to distract me from that.

By this point, by the time of my finals at RADA, I was going through a major change; finally growing up after leaving home, losing my accent, changing my posture, developing my own personality, forming my own views and all the rest of it. But, in reality, I was probably very mixed up.

It was very strange going home, back to Ilkeston. It got worse and worse each time because suddenly people were looking at me as if I was a bit of a weirdo. I dressed like a typical student at the time, which probably didn't help. I was playing the student part to the full and, as it was all very hippy-dippy then, had the long hair, Afghan coat, desert boots and spoke fluent flower-power.

I remember my dad coming to meet me at Nottingham station on one trip home. I was coming back for a summer break and was quite excited at the prospect, not least for the chance of a good meal. By that time, dungarees, flat caps, collarless shirts and boots had become fashionable among students. There I was arriving at Nottingham station and, as I got off the train with my bag, Dad exclaimed, "What the bloody 'ell are you dressed as?" I said, "This is it. This is what I wear." He said, "You look like a bloody coal miner." What was happening, of course, was that students were playing the opposite of what was expected of them. They were trying to be more 'of the people'. My dad expected me to come back home wearing a cravat whereas there we all were in London, dressing down and being 'terribly terribly' with it.

RADA took up two years of my life, from 1968 to 1970. I try to think now if it was a great time for me or not. All I can say is that I don't really know. Although I do have good memories of RADA and that part of my life, I've got fonder memories of Clarendon. I've kept in touch with a lot more people from Clarendon, mainly because that was before the 'change' as I think of it. I feel now that I just didn't know who I was at RADA. All I knew was that I wanted to go from there into work and to become a successful actor. I was told that the only way I could do that was by changing my accent, but I didn't realise that it was going to change my entire personality.

It wasn't just the accent; it was the Alexander Technique to change my posture and all the other influences. One minute I'd be talking 'yer kno', greyt, greyt' – very eager and wide-eyed with the flat vowels, and all of a sudden I was speaking 'terribly like that'. I even smoked in a rather Noel Coward kind of way and, bizarrely, started wearing glasses with plain lenses to make me look more intellectual. Oh God, what a poser I must have looked. I can picture myself even now and I squirm with embarrassment at the image. But somewhere in the middle of all this there was still the working-class rebel. I certainly had a bit of a chip on my shoulder, although I'm not quite sure why as I wasn't brought up that way by my parents. Perhaps it was a personality that I developed to protect myself from all these changes that were being thrown at me. However, the determination to achieve something was certainly there and I knew I had to change in order to succeed.

Let's face it, I couldn't have made a career out of doing just Midlands character parts and I'm always amazed now at young actors who have retained their accents but have the ability to change their voice at will. Oh well, *c'est la vie* – as Noel Coward must surely have once said. Poser!

You also have to imagine me, a former sewer worker at an ironworks in the East Midlands, making his first venture out of a changing room in his first pair of ballet tights and pumps – the embarrassment was made somewhat easier to deal with because everyone else was in the same situation and there was definitely a feeling that no one was to laugh at anyone else. We had entered into the world of one of the most eccentric movement teachers at RADA – Madame Fedra. She was then in her mid to late sixties, yet still very beautiful, and had a commanding presence, speaking with rich Russian vowels. "Vell my darhlings," she would say, "I am now going to teach you to move, you vill follow me." She then proceeded to walk the length of the room and, of course, I was singled out to copy her.

"No my darhling, you must move from the bawlls."

"I'm sorry Madame – from the bowels?"

"No my darhling – the *bawlls*," she repeated as she pointed her stick at my testicles. Billy Elliott never had to suffer this indignity! Fortunately for me, she then moved on to her next victim – a wonderful actress called Lynn Dearth – who I have to say looked even worse than I did in tights.

"My darhling, can you type?"

"Yes Madame, I can."

"Good, because you're going to need to when you leave here."

Madame Fedra was just one of many extraordinary teachers during Hugh Cruttwell's period as principal of RADA. Others included Ben Bennison – my mime teacher, David Perry, Judith Gick and Gilbert Vernon. I adored them and shall forever be in their debt.

I don't think any drama school can properly prepare you for the realities of the theatrical profession although RADA, at that time, really did give me a sense of what theatre was all about. I suspect that all my posing and pretensions, although I laugh at them now, served me well.

I'm only in contact with a few of the students who were at RADA with me; very few actually. Of course when we left on that final hot summer's day in July 1970, we were all sobbing and saying we'd keep in touch. But, as is the way of these things – particularly in our profession – that didn't happen.

Most of us had secured an agent from our showcase finals and were all moving on from the safety and security of our school to the exciting world of acting.

At that time, in the final two terms, the principal selected various roles and plays to showcase your particular talent to the public and a group of agents. I had stressed to Hugh Cruttwell that I didn't want to do a George Bernard Shaw. So what did he put me in? *Major Barbara*.

However, after one of the finals productions that I actually wanted to be in, Congreve's *Love for Love*, an agent called Marina Martin left me her card. That was what agents did then. They left their cards with a scribbled note on saying 'Please call'. They'd leave it in your pigeonhole. I remember seeing Marina and thinking she was stunning. I ran out onto the street as she was walking away, chasing after her and saying "hello" in an awful Leslie Phillips kind of way. She just turned round and said, "I didn't mean you needed to see me now. I meant for you to give me a call. Just call me, we shouldn't discuss it here."

I'd heard of Marina as an agent, but I didn't realise she was with a big agency, CCA (which still exists), set up by Howard Pays. She became my first agent and got me an audition for the Northcott Theatre in Exeter. It was my first professional audition. Fortunately, I got in straight away. I was off to Devon; moving on, letting go.

FIVE

THE BIG BANG

IN EXETER, Tony Church, an ex-Royal Shakespeare Company actor, was in the midst of his last season as artistic director at the Northcott Theatre. Before he left, he took me on in an acting/assistant stage manager role for the company, and so I was accordingly given a mixture of performing and stage management duties to fulfil.

The first play I was involved in – and my first professional play as a performer – was *The Roses of Eyam* by Don Taylor, a work that I appeared in again when it was adapted for television.

It was about the great plague in Derbyshire, my home ground. But, of course, I'd just lost the accent! I'd spent two years losing my authentic Derbyshire voice and suddenly I had to call it back. When I did, it just sounded fake. I was meant to be coaching the other actors in the accent, sound, intonation and speech patterns, and even they were going, "That doesn't sound right!"

Originally I was only hired to do a twelve-week season at the Northcott, but just as I was about to leave, Jane Howell from London's Royal Court Theatre was appointed as artistic director and asked me to stay on. I said yes immediately. It proved to be a big turning point in my life. Jane was a very committed left-wing Brechtian and into very serious political theatre. She came down to Exeter with the intention of forming a permanent company of twenty or so actors; she only kept five actors from Tony Church's band of players – one of them being me.

Jane brought some great people to the company. There was Hayden Griffin, famous as the designer on various Edward Bond plays, director Bill Gaskill, writer Howard Brenton and Edward Bond himself.

The theatre was located within Exeter University, which was incredibly middle class. No one from inside or outside the university was really interested in political theatre – it just wasn't that kind of campus. They were more about cream teas on a Sunday and a glass of cider in the evenings. It was all very tame and unadventurous. However, it was fantastic for me because the theatre we were doing took me back to my roots. It got me thinking about where I came from and who I was. I found that I was actually quite left wing; that I was quite committed to the issues we were broaching. We did a fantastic show about pollution, which we also toured around the region, and I remember feeling then, in 1971/2, that I was in tune with the politics of the play.

The touring company visited venues that were part of the South West Arts Association. We did a lot of small places, but also some bigger theatres like the Bristol Old Vic, the Theatre Royal in Bath and the New Theatre in Cardiff.

Touring also took in the Minack Theatre in Cornwall, now a major venue. As you may know, it's an open-air theatre right on the sea's edge. It was founded by Rowena Cade, a fellow Derbyshire native and a real character, who I got to know very well. She was instrumental in getting the Minack built – she even had each stone seat engraved with the name of a production. Sadly, Rowena died some years ago but is now justly famous.

Performing at the Minack was a wonderful experience and we had an idyllic routine there. After finishing a matinee we'd go down to dive off the rocks and spend the afternoon on the beach, before climbing back up the cliffs to the dressing rooms where we'd get ready for the evening performances, which were always packed. The play would go on whatever the weather because people would come prepared for all conditions.

It's also the only theatre I know where a fish can steal the show. On one particular day, a fifteen-foot-long basking shark turned up in the bay. Its arrival caused major consternation along the beaches and people came from miles away to see it. Of course, the show at the Minack went on regardless… well almost. I was half way through a speech when the audience suddenly, unexpectedly, applauded. I thought at first that it was for me and my performance, but then quickly realised that no one was actually looking at me. I followed the gaze of the audience, looked behind me and saw that the basking shark had performed a little dive! That's what they were all standing up to applaud. Upstaged by a shark!

The South West was such a wonderful area to be in, and I spent two very happy and contented years down there. My family – my mum, dad, brother and sister – would come down and have their holidays in Cornwall and Devon, staying on a campsite while we were touring nearby. The summers were just bliss because even in Exeter you were only a few miles from a beach… and then there were beautiful villages like Topsham and the wild moorland a few miles to the west. Happy memories indeed.

At that time acting wasn't an open shop. The big thing was that you had to 'earn your weeks' to get your blue Equity card, otherwise you couldn't make your living as an actor. I was working on getting my ticket into the profession, and being part of the Northcott Company was crucial to achieving that, crucial to becoming a professional actor. I began with a provisional, red Equity card and then had to do twenty-six weeks to get my full blue card.

It was during that period, not long after finishing at RADA, that I changed my name. In the stage version of *The Roses of Eyam*, I think I was still Robert L Stevenson, but then Equity asked me to change it to avoid confusion with other similar names on their books: there was a choreographer called Bob Stevenson, the actor Robert Stephens, and a film director for Walt Disney called Robert Stevenson. Equity said it might be in my best interests to change my name, so I just used my middle name for a surname and became Robert Lindsay. In truth, it didn't feel like a dramatic shift – the accent, the posture and everything else, that all did much more to cloud my sense of identity.

I am not aware of any family history to the name Lindsay – it was given to me by my mum (thank God my dad didn't have his way or my middle name would have been Louis). At least it meant I could use my own names rather than having to make something up. When I got my full Equity card, which was considered a big thing then, and became a proper professional actor during Jane Howell's first season at Northcott, I emerged as Robert Lindsay.

Although the change of name was fairly easy for me, some of my contemporaries at RADA would suddenly turn up with the daftest names. There was a noticeboard where you had to 'clock in' every morning to show that you were in attendance. This went on in a fairly straightforward way for two years until the term of our finals, when we were looking for agents, and you'd suddenly be greeted by the most amazing names like Ambro Silk, Honey Greensmith, Nathan Blain-Wright, Swanton Morley, Turner Shelton, Liberty Cosgrave, Walter Wilbrahams and so on. In truth, I've changed the real made-up names to protect the guilty, but sheer invention was obviously the way to go!

On one occasion, Bosun – the main greeter at RADA – was busy on the phone directing callers to the speech department with a broad cockney accent, "'Ang on mate, puttin' you frew to speech now." I said to him, as I was looking up at the notice-board, "Sorry to interrupt you, Bosun, but what's happened to all my classmates. Have they left?"

"No, they've changed their ruddy names – and it's 'ard enough findin' people as it is. Bloody actors. Ponces."

So, back to the Northcott Theatre. The first production of Jane Howell's tenure there was a major, controversial version of *Measure for Measure* in which they played the Duke as Harold Macmillan and the other main character, Angelo, as Enoch Powell. All the lawyers came down from London to see it. Unfortunately, pretty much nobody else did.

The problem was that, as I've indicated, hardly anyone came to the theatre at all because of its location in the middle of the university. Theatre-going obviously wasn't on the students' agenda. The actual institution of the university didn't seem particularly interested in us either at that time and, although the drama department eventually started linking up with the the-atre, to begin with there was no participation by it or its students.

The rest of Northcott's potential audience lived out 'in the sticks' and going to the theatre seemed to be too much effort for them.

That was the setting for Jane. When she went ahead and created this working-class, 'power to the people' style of theatre, no one came; the place was empty. Of course we, the company, thought that it was 'right-on' theatre and loved it.

One night at the Northcott really sticks in my mind. It was the opening night of the Edward Bond play *Narrow Road to the Deep North*. While the local audience stayed away in droves, Jane's politicised style of drama had actually caused a significant stir within the theatre world. So much so in fact that lots of people came down from London to see the show, drawn by her Royal Court connections.

We gave them a show to remember. First of all the roof fell in. It wasn't that we'd 'brought the house down', it was a little more mundane: the ceiling physically collapsed into the auditorium, delaying the start of the show. Plaster came down and covered the audience in dust, so we had to clear the mess up and then get the audience cleaned up. As a result, we were half an hour late with curtain up.

I was playing the Cannoneer and, in one scene, I had to fire this huge cannon. I mean it was vast – a Hayden Griffin special. In the back of the programme there was a special notice about it, warning the audience that there would be a loud 'report'. Those of a nervous disposition or with similar problems were told that they should 'please be advised that a sudden loud bang' would occur. So, the audience knew, and were fully primed that when the big gun came on they should start preparing for the cannon's roar. You could sense the audience bracing in nervous anticipation.

So, the cannon was wheeled out and pulled onto the stage. All the cast were sitting there and I was crouched behind the cannon, waiting for the big moment.

I shouted: "FIRE!"

Nothing! It didn't go off. I could see the cast wincing and squirming. Again I shouted: "FIRE!"

And again, silence!

The tension was unbearable. Eventually some bright spark (excuse the pun) shouted, "BANG!" Exeunt omnes except for a solitary Cannoneer.

I looked around and I was alone on stage; the cast had walked off and abandoned me. I could hear muffled shrieks of laughter in the wings. There I was, alone on stage with an unfired cannon and an entire audience still holding its breath, waiting for the moment they had been warned about. The lights went down, I walked off stage – it was an early interval.

Backstage, everyone in the cast was crying with laughter. Apart from Jane. She came storming in. "You bastards. All of you. You've ruined my f***ing career. Do you realise how important this night is?" But the cast were just too convulsed with laughter to stop. As she got to the top of her yelling, the cannon suddenly went off and yet more of the ceiling came down, adding to the hysteria. Oh God! It was all we could do to go back on.

It seems extraordinary that someone as politically motivated as Jane Howell, with her Royal Court background, came to be working in such a middle-class theatre. Her intentions were extremely honourable and she taught me one major thing: yes, of course theatre is about being popular – you need to get bums on seats – but the work must also have creative integrity and come from your heart and soul, even if it sometimes fails.

It's something you must believe in. My period at the Northcott really gave me a sense that it's not easy to please everyone, but as long as the work comes from yourself, it's probably the most rewarding experience when it *is* successful. When this happens, it pushes you on to make it happen again. Obviously, as I get older, work is governed by so many other factors but one of Jane's comments to me as I left Exeter has remained true: "Trust your instinct and remember the first time you read something is the most important."

1. At seven months old.
My mother taught us all to smile!

2. Andrew and Lorraine, my
younger brother and sister.
By this point, I was already
preparing to leave home.

3. The garden at Larklands Avenue where my imagination took flight.

4. On holiday with Mum and Dad whilst recuperating from TB – sorry, pneumonia! I refused to be photographed in a wheelchair.

5. Running in the sea at Mablethorpe – James Bond eat your heart out!

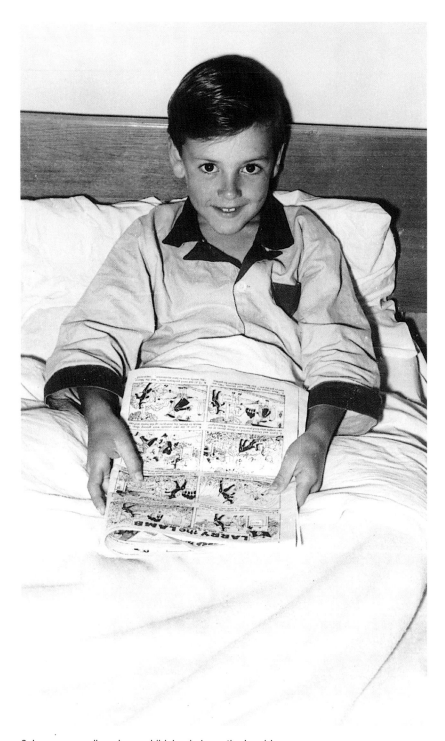

6. I was very well read as a child. Look, Larry the Lamb!

7. Me with Dad (right) and future 'London Dad' Uncle Harry.

8. Jesse Stevenson, the grandfather I never knew, who survived the trenches only to die of TB in his fifties.

9. Granddad Dunmore who was blown up at Gallipoli in the First World War which is why he was stone deaf.

10. Grandma Stevenson (left) and Grandma Dunmore (right) desperately tried to save me from a life-changing beating.

11. Lorraine with Uncle Mac – the inspiration for my Archie Rice (the man, not my sister!).

12. Mum and Dad – my role models for a happy marriage.
They were so in love for so many years.

13. At Gladstone Secondary Modern Boys' School. How did I avoid being chained up and thrown down the school steps?

14. Playing the Pied Piper at Gladstone Boys' – my first stage role. I look so much like my son Sam does now!

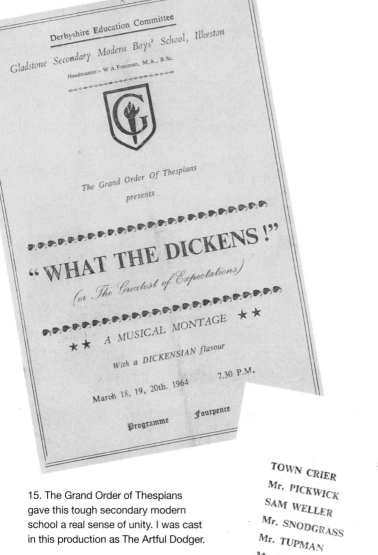

Derbyshire Education Committee

Gladstone Secondary Modern Boys' School, Ilkeston

Headmaster:- W.A.Freeman, M.A., B.Sc.

G

The Grand Order Of Thespians

presents

"WHAT THE DICKENS !"

(or The Greatest of Expectations)

★★ A MUSICAL MONTAGE ★★

With a DICKENSIAN flavour

March 18, 19, 20th. 1964   7.30 P.M.

Programme   Fourpence

15. The Grand Order of Thespians gave this tough secondary modern school a real sense of unity. I was cast in this production as The Artful Dodger.

CAST
★★★★★

TOWN CRIER	John Aldred
Mr. PICKWICK	Owen Smith
SAM WELLER	Michael Brown
Mr. SNODGRASS	Kevin Doar
Mr. TUPMAN	Malcolm Chambers
Mr. WINKLE	Paul Lebeter
FAGIN	
OLIVER TWIST	David Raszka
CHARLIE BATES	Desmond Eyre
The ARTFUL DODGER	Ivan Bostock
ALFIE DORKER	Robert Stevenson
BILL SIKES	Kenneth Limb
WORKHOUSE MASTER	Norman Swift
Mr. BUMBLE	Kevin Lewis
JACK	Alan Trowman
	Dai Smith

WORKHOUSE BOYS

Gary Andrews   David Black
George Cranage   Brian Goscoigne   Roy Burley
David Perry   Michael Roe   Roy Knighton
Roger Smith   Gary Slaney

16. The great man, John Lally, who first recognised my talent as a performer. He was quite a performer himself!

17. *A Hatful of Rain* at Clarendon College. Boy, did I have attitude (centre)!

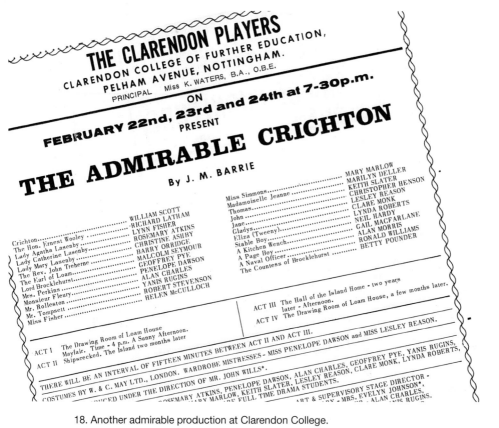

THE CLARENDON PLAYERS

CLARENDON COLLEGE OF FURTHER EDUCATION,
PELHAM AVENUE, NOTTINGHAM.

PRINCIPAL   Miss K. WATERS, B.A., O.B.E.

ON

FEBRUARY 22nd, 23rd and 24th at 7-30p.m.

PRESENT

THE ADMIRABLE CRICHTON

By J. M. BARRIE

Crichton.. WILLIAM SCOTT
The Hon. Ernest Wooley .... RICHARD LATHAM
Lady Agatha Lasenby....................... LYNN FISHER
Lady Catherine Lasenby.................... ROSEMARY ATKINS
Lady Mary Lasenby .... CHRISTINE ASHBY
The Rev. John Treherne .... BARRY ORRIDGE
The Earl of Loam............................. MALCOLM SEYMOUR
Lord Brocklehurst............................. GEOFFREY PYE
Mrs. Perkins .... PENELOPE DAWSON
Monsieur Fleury .... ALAN CHARLES
Mr. Rolleston .... YANIS RUGINS
Mr. Tompsett .... ROBERT STEVENSON
Miss Fisher .... HELEN McCULLOCH

Miss Simmons.................................. MARY MARLOW
Madamoiselle Jeanne .... MARILYN DELLER
Thomas.. KEITH SLATER
John .... CHRISTOPHER HENSON
Jane .... LESLEY REASON
Gladys... CLARE MONK
Eliza (Tweeny)................................. LYNDA ROBERTS
Stable Boy.. NEIL HARDY
A Kitchen Wench.............................. GAIL MACFARLANE
A Page Boy .... ALAN MORRIS
A Naval Officer .... RONALD WILLIAMS
The Countess of Brocklehurst .... BETTY POUNDER

ACT III   The Hall of the Island Home - two years
          later - Afternoon.
ACT IV   The Drawing Room of Loam House, a few months later.

ACT I   The Drawing Room of Loam House
        Mayfair.   Time - 4 p.m. A Sunny Afternoon.
ACT II Shipwrecked. The Island two months later

THERE WILL BE AN INTERVAL OF FIFTEEN MINUTES BETWEEN ACT II AND ACT III.

COSTUMES BY W. & C. MAY LTD., LONDON. WARDROBE MISTRESSES - MISS PENELOPE DAWSON and MISS LESLEY REASON.

PRODUCED UNDER THE DIRECTION OF MR. JOHN WILLS*.

.... ROSEMARY ATKINS, PENELOPE DAWSON, ALAN CHARLES, GEOFFREY PYE, YANIS RUGINS,
.... MARLOW, KEITH SLATER, LESLEY REASON, CLARE MONK, LYNDA ROBERTS,
.... ARE FULL TIME DRAMA STUDENTS.

.... ART & SUPERVISORY STAGE DIRECTOR -
...... BY - MRS. EVELYN JOHNSON*,
.... ALAN CHARLES,
....IS RUGINS.

18. Another admirable production at Clarendon College.

19. Joining RADA.

20. Leaving RADA – my first 10x8 publicity still. Two years' acting from the 'bowels' – what a transformation!

21. *Letter From a Soldier* – an early TV appearance. I even had to a wear a false tash.

22. In *Journey's End* (centre) with Anthony Dutton (left) and Michael Cadman (right).

born in 1880 in Manhattan
and fought in the Spanish-
30. Returning from the Army, he
He became an alcoholic, but
a leading newspaper
his reputation there that he
New York American' in
ports writer, sometimes
, as when he accompanied
ld War I.

e twilight circles of
way with an ease
isten to anyone, and
world-famous for
o other film
or successes
her the guys
r not. In
steps' by
idents
beyond
refined
came as
s
rowd.

GUYS AND DOLLS

Nicely-Nicely Johnson
Benny Southstreet
Rusty Charlie
Nathan Detroit
Miss Adelaide
Sky Masterton
Sarah Brown
Big Jule
Harry the Horse
Lieut. Brannigan
Arvide Abernathy
General Matilda B. Cartwright
Agatha in Mission Band
Hot Box Girls

DAVID PEART
ROBERT LINDSAY
BRIAN PROTHEROE
NEIL McLAUCHLAN
JOANNA TOPE
BRIAN CAPRON
JANETTE LEGGE
ROY MARSDEN
RHYS MARSDEN
NICK BRIMBLE
MICHAEL SCHOLES
JANET DALE
HAZEL CLYNE
DIANA RAWORTH
HAZEL CLYNE
JANET DALE
JOHN DICKS
MYLES REITHERMANN
RAY BARCIA

Liver Lips Louie
Society Max
Angie the Ox

MUSICIANS
Alto Saxophone /Clarinet
Tenor Saxophone /Clarinet
Trumpet
Trumpet
Trombone
Piano
Bass
Drums
Rehearsal Pianist

John Plant or Ken Rockett
Paul Bridgewater
Tony Huxham) or Alan Hempstead,Arthur
John Glanfield) Vann & Barry Dennidge
Lewis Huxham or Owen Huxham
Cass Hope
William Kerr
Derek Sargeant
Cass Hope

THERE WILL BE ONE INTERVAL OF 15 MINUTES

GUYS AND DOLLS opening night Wednesday
Running in repertoire with HAPPY FAM

23. The programme from *Guys and Dolls* at Exeter's Northcott Theatre.

24. The cast of *Guys and Dolls* and Jane Howell's permanent company, photographed in the grounds of the university (I'm on the far right!).

25. In *That'll Be the Day* with David Essex and my terrible beard!

26. *That'll Be the Day* again. Oh bugger me!

27. The cast of the musical *Godspell* (I'm front right) – none of them dared tell me that the show had received its notice.

28. In *Three For All* with Billy Beethoven, the band that never was. I wonder why? (From left to right) Paul Nicholas, me, Simon Williams and Chris Neil with (front) Graham Bonnet.

29. As Tom in *Three For All*. The drummer
from Showaddywaddy (who also appeared
in the film) loved my kit but was a little
bemused that I couldn't actually play it!

30. *Get Some In* – at last I got to play the rocker.

31. As Jakey Smith in *Get Some In* with Tony Selby. "Is that one 'f' or two?"

32. Wolfie in *Citizen Smith*. 'Power to the People'
– but who's playing who?

33. The Tooting Popular Front out on manoeuvres in a stolen tank. My friend Mike Grady is the one on the left.

34. With Mum and Dad at my wedding to Cheryl Hall. "You're making the biggest mistake of your life," Dad whispered.

35. Performing (right) in *A Midsummer Night's Dream*. The bad BBC wig would go back to the cupboard on its own when I whistled!

36. 'Sparring' with Alan Minter in preparation for the BBC comedy series *Seconds Out*.

37. Playing Iachimo in *Cymbeline* with Helen Mirren (centre) and Richard Johnson (seated left).

38. Playing Hamlet directed by Braham Murray at the Royal Exchange Theatre, Manchester. We chose to perform the production without lighting or period costumes.

39. Give Us A Break with Paul McGann.

40. Playing Edmund in *King Lear* with Diana Rigg as Regan.

SIX

ME, RINGO, ESSEX AND THE MOON

I WAS still in Exeter in 1971 when Marina Martin, my agent, came down to see me with a casting director, Celestia Sporborg, in tow.

Celestia was casting for the movie *That'll Be the Day* and I was put forward for a part. I wanted to play a cool Teddy boy but the part I got, Terry, turned out to be a dismally dull character. Surrounded by all those cool people, there I was playing the nerd. So after two years' classical training, acting from the 'bowels', then two more years in Brechtian theatre playing in everything from *Narrow Road to the Deep North* to *Galileo*, I was about to be in a rock film playing a grammar school twit.

Even before it came out, *That'll Be the Day* stirred up major press attention. Filming was to take place on the Isle of Wight and they were going to seal virtually the whole island off from the public – God knows how. And the reason it was treated as such a major event was because David Essex – heart-throb *du jour* back in 1971 – had the starring role in his first big film.

There were some very cool people in that film, playing very

cool parts. Ringo Starr was a fairground Teddy boy, Billy Fury was playing an old rocker called Stormy Tempest, and Keith Moon was a crazy drummer (what are the chances?). It was the place to be and the film to be in. But what did I get? Terry, a puffed-up grammar school twit who said "bugger me" every time he appeared. I had my head shaved and they put pimples and acne on my face. They even made my ears stick out! I mean I was, like, *so* not cool. And all the time I was walking around surrounded by every gorgeous groupie in the world. How unfair was that?

It was a rock film alright. A rock film with its rocks off. Right at the start I was introduced to Keith Moon in the corridor of the hotel, a bottle of brandy in one hand, a young lady in the other.

The First (first assistant on the film), Garth Thomas, a very famous First, had met me when I arrived. He collected me at the steps of the Shanklin Hotel and said, "Come on in. Have a drink." I was carrying two huge suitcases, but the next thing I knew I was drinking this large glass of something. I still don't know what it was. Walking along a corridor, he goes "Keith, Keith, er… this is Robert Lindsay." Keith Moon, turning to look over his shoulder, says "Ello mate" then turns away to carry on.

You could smell 'weed' everywhere; the atmosphere was thick with the stuff, as if the hotel itself was floating above its foundations. I suppose this was my first real experience of the big time, my awakening if you like.

I went to my room, which was big and fabulous and overlooked the ocean. The next thing I knew a girl came in who introduced herself as Polly, David Puttnam's personal assistant (David was producing the film). I put my bags down and she took my hand and led me out to a party on the beach. I had my first real marijuana experience, my first joint, on that beach. I'd had a puff at RADA, but never to any real effect. I'd always pretended I was stoned, because in truth I was terrified of the stuff. But that night I got completely blitzed out of my mind and ended up in bed with a couple of girls. This was my first night on my first major film.

That party on the beach could have been a movie in itself. Every rock god you could think of was down there. The next morning I found out that most of the film crew were on penicillin as they'd got a massive dose of the clap and were off the alcohol.

One evening the hotel staged a fashion show – a very blue-rinse fashion show. All the old ladies of Shanklin had come to the hotel and were in its conference room. It was very 'ladies of C&A'. The rockers and I arrived back at the hotel and – for a laugh I suppose – we went into the fashion show clutching our drinks. The next thing I saw was a completely naked Keith Moon walking on with the models. He was parading down the catwalk without a stitch on. The old ladies loved him! They didn't boo – they cheered. He charmed the pants of those old dears. Or had they charmed the pants off him?

I was amazed at the danger of Keith Moon. And yet, the thing was, he was quite a nice bloke underneath all that. It was all an act. He was very insecure. He had to be noticed. He had to be the centre of attention and he was certainly that alright, fully clothed or not.

Normally I went back to the mainland for the weekend if I was free and wasn't filming on the Monday, but on one particular Friday I decided to stay, because David Essex was throwing a party in a local restaurant. As the evening drew on they all began playing instruments – the piano, ukeleles and stuff. And what did I do? I played the spoons! There I was in the middle of 'When you're smiling, when you're smiling, the whole world smiles with you…' with two legendary drummers saying, "Oh man, it's great. Great man, wow." I was teaching them how to play the spoons! Oh bugger me!

Ringo was so charming; a really gentle, nice guy and, actually, in my opinion, a very underrated actor. I think he was very good in *That'll Be the Day*. He played the whizz-kid on the waltzer, short-changing everyone, including 'Bugger-me'.

That'll Be the Day was a major, major event in my life for all sorts of reasons, not least because it was my first real experience of film, of working in front of the camera. I didn't have a clue what I was doing. For instance, when I was filming a scene with Rosemary Leach, who was playing David Essex's mother and with whom I've since worked on *My Family*, they'd built tracks for the camera all the way down the street. The camera came down on a 'railway' track and I walked towards Rosemary, knowing that I had to step over the track and give my line. And they said: "No, no, no… Cut! We can see you walking over the track." "Well," I said, "that's because it's a railway track!" "No, no," they explained. "You see, the thing is, you don't look at the track." And there's me, taking a big step, going "bugger me", as per my character's stock phrase.

They yelled, "No! Cut! Robert… don't look!" I reacted with: "How can I walk and not step over?" "Just look at her, 'feel' it and just glide across the track." So, then what happens? What do I do? I go arse over tit. That's what happens. I actually caught my foot in the railway track, tripped over it and knocked into the camera. They had to catch the camera. A quarter of a million pounds worth of equipment sent flying!

It was literally a crash course in acting in front of and to the camera. Claude Whatham, the film's director, was very intense, completely focused on trying to make it all happen. He was probably slightly *too* intense as I gather he almost had a nervous breakdown after it. He was trying to keep it all together and they were all just being reckless around him.

I'm grateful to Claude for the way he mentored me in the art of acting in front of a camera, explaining the subtleties of technique to someone who was used to the theatre. I don't remember doing any film or television preparation work at RADA as it was essentially voice and theatre training; all – you know – breathing, fencing and a very large, expansive performance, all gearing you up for the theatre. At that time there were films being made in the UK but not in any great quantity, and TV opportunities were few and far between. As a result, I'd had no experience of working in front of a camera at all and controlling my facial expressions. The problem with me is that I have such a 'big' face! It took me years to work out that the 'smaller' I keep my face, the more interesting it is. I look back at *That'll Be the Day* and think 'just calm down'!

I can't use the excuse that I was just being expressive. Looking back at that whole early period it was, in fact, overacting on my part, and I guess it wasn't until I started doing the early sit-coms in the 1970s that I properly understood why.

Part of the problem was that English actors at that time were primed to go onto the stage, where *the* big influence in everyone's lives was Laurence Olivier. He was a man of great versatility, but was predominantly theatre trained and, as such, he was very, very expansive as an actor. He gave huge performances and, because his was the level that we all aspired to, that was what you thought you had to do. Nevertheless, Olivier was one of the few stage actors who could do film and television successfully. Even while some of his filmed Shakespeares are big 'theatre' performances, other films like *Rebecca*, for example, are studies in subtlety.

I got paid five hundred pounds for my role as 'Bugger-me' Terry, almost all of which I immediately spent on buying David Puttnam's car, a black Mini Cooper. Can you imagine? I went down to the car park under the hotel to see it. He wanted £380 for it and I bought it straight away. In total, I was on the Isle of Wight for about ten weeks and although I had days off, I was there for the whole thing. When my contract came to an end, the first big problem was figuring out where I was going to live. My time in Exeter had finished so I couldn't go back there, but I didn't really know what I was going to do next. At least by this point I had my full Equity card.

I went back to London and dossed around in old mates' apartments. For a time I shacked up with a girl who had been starring at the Northcott. I went to stay with her and it turned into a relationship, which was silly because really she was just providing me with somewhere to stay – it shouldn't have gone any further but the old insecurity problem had raised its ugly head yet again. That got me into very deep water until I moved on after about eight or nine months and went to stay in Islington with an old friend from RADA. I'd be in London all week and would go home at weekends, back to Nottingham and some real food.

The next move was that three of us – John Dicks, Tony Allen and myself – all actors and all homeless – agreed to work concertedly to find an apartment we could share. We managed to rent Tony Church's apartment right on Hampstead Heath. It was a four-bedroomed, second-floor apartment. It was huge! We lived there for a year and a half, while Tony, who had given me my first theatre job, was at the RSC in Stratford with his family, having rented a house up there. It was the Church family who gave me my first base. Suddenly I was really living in London, with my own room and my own phone – things were beginning to fall into place.

SEVEN

PLAYING JESUS

I STILL had my agent, Marina Martin, and she was still sending me up for auditions. I managed to get a job at the Belgrade Theatre in Coventry doing *Journey's End*, the RC Sherriff play set in the First World War trenches. I shared a flat with Simon Mac-Corkindale and we certainly enjoyed ourselves, what with *The Val Doonican Show* and all its chorus girls just down the road. We were far worse than Paddy McGinty's goat! Every time I see Simon now, which, unfortunately, is very rarely, he says to me, "Remember Coventry? And they *send* you to Coventry!?"

The Belgrade employed an English actress called Patricia Cutts. I'd never heard of her but apparently she'd gone out to Hollywood and become something of a starlet. She was a reckless human being, and very fond of a drink or two. It was her first time back from the movies in LA, and she was at the theatre to do a Terence Rattigan play, *A Bequest to the Nation*. I played Nelson as a young boy, but it was all about Nelson as an old boy! All flashbacks. I didn't have much to do in it, but alternated that role with playing Raleigh in *Journey's End*. Patricia didn't have much stage experience and we didn't know whether it was that or her other problems that made her performances rather strange and unpredictable. The set was made up of large suspended picture frames and fixed doorways. She used to lean on the picture frames making them wobble and never entered the scene through the doorway as she was supposed to. This would set the audience giggling and exasperate the rest of us. She turned out to be a rather tragic case – she was found dead a year later, aged forty-eight, apparently having committed suicide.

By this time I was well and truly Robert Lindsay. My first big job with the new name was the last thing that I did at Exeter, a production of *Guys and Dolls* directed by David Toguri. That was also the job where I found my singing voice.

I played Benny Southstreet. "We got the horse right here…" That's Benny, he sings that. And we all sang: "When you see a guy reach for stars in the sky…" which was the show's big number. David went on to work on the big national production, but ours also got quite a bit of attention. It was a very successful show – very well done, in the manner of a strip-cartoon. In essence they *are* like cartoon characters and I'm sure it would make a good graphic novel in today's terms.

Once I'd done *Guys and Dolls* I realised I could sing; realised that, actually, I really enjoyed this singing lark. It marked a real change from how I'd felt at RADA, where there was a teacher who pooh-poohed me as a singer. He didn't even have a proper room, just a place for his piano in a corridor – that's how tight for space RADA was. They had music lessons for students but he wouldn't take me. I don't think he saw any singing potential in me, which was a shame in retrospect because I missed out on two years of good musical training there.

As a consequence, I hadn't had any formal singing lessons before I sang on stage for the first time in *Guys and Dolls*. I hadn't really sung at school (and not much even in the bathroom at home!). The most I had done was to mime to The Beatles at some school event where we did 'Twist and Shout' and my group won it! On another occasion I'd 'performed' rather than sung Gilbert and Sullivan's 'I am the very model of a modern Major-General...' song. But that was about it, that was the extent of my singing experience.

Then came *Guys and Dolls* with complicated harmonies and descants going on. It had a fantastic musical director – Del Newman. "You gotta great voice," he said to me, turning round from the piano. *He* was the one who encouraged me to think of myself as a singer, the one who got me started in musicals. After that, I did *Godspell* a year later and, in musical terms, I was up and running.

Although *Guys and Dolls* was my first singing part, it didn't make me extra-nervous. In fact – do you know what? – nerves have never figured in my stage career, ever. I've been lucky in that respect. Some actors routinely throw up before a performance (or even during it, if their timing's particularly bad), but I've always been okay.

Even though I felt quite natural with the mechanics of singing and with doing a singing role, I still had to work at it quite a bit. Once I'd left Exeter, and was living in London with John and Tony, I began going to a singing coach called Chuck Mallett and he used to play for me at auditions.

Unfortunately I hadn't started going to Chuck when I went up for an audition for *Grease*. In fact you could say that audition proved instrumental in me seeking out Chuck's expertise. Richard

Gere was up for the same audition. It was the first UK stage production of *Grease* and was way before the film version was made.

I went along to the audition at the Mermaid Theatre and watched people walking on with their guitars and doing Elvis impersonations and God knows what else. I sat on a bench and watched Richard Gere audition. You could see even then that the guy was going places. At that time he was just some bloke from LAMDA or somewhere, but he was obviously American and so had that to his advantage, as well as being obviously kinda hip and cool, with the tight Levis and the whole bit.

Imagine how I felt, having just played 'Bugger-me' Terry in *That'll Be the Day*. I'd only just regrown my hair into some kind of Beatles mop-top style after they shaved it off for the film. I must have still looked awful, but I don't think I fully realised it at the time because I wanted to be glamorous like everyone else. I clambered onto the stage for my audition, ready with two songs that I'd prepared, one of which was:

'You're so young and beautiful and I love you so,
Your lips so red, your eyes that shine...'

I got half way through and this American voice from the stalls called out: "Robert! Bob! Could you stop, please?"

I said: "Yeah! Sorry. Problem?"

He replied: " Yeah, that's 'Young and Beautiful' right?"

Me: "Yeah."

"You're singing it to the tune of 'Wooden Heart'."

I'd got the lyrics mixed up. And that, as they say, was the end of that. I didn't get that musical. I'll leave you to guess who did!

Something had to be done. I'd never used a voice or vocal coach until someone after the *Grease* audition said to me, "You need singing lessons – you need to wise up." That struck a chord, you might say, after what had happened. So I rang this guy Chuck Mallett, as recommended by a friend. He had a lovely apartment in Pimlico, a place that seemed to have a revolving door of famous people going in and out for hourly lessons throughout the day. You were in for an hour, then out and off. Elaine Paige (also in that first production of *Grease*) would go in and come out, followed minutes later by someone like Millicent Martin from *That Was The Week That Was*. I recognised every one of his pupils as someone famous, so I knew this guy was 'hot'.

He was a very lovely, very gay Canadian guy, immensely sweet but also incredibly stern about breathing and about choice of song. He'd get very impatient if you chose something really modern to sing. For example, I got completely fixated by Don McLean's 'Vincent', as everyone else did at the time:

'Starry, starry night,
Paint your palette blue and grey...'

A hopeless song to sing, unless you're Don McLean!

It would take Chuck to say, "It's not your song. It doesn't fit. Let's go with something from a musical." Chuck was very good with me, so helpful. He started to groom me, encouraging with the odd Canadian "yeah!" when things went right. Actually, he gave me a lot of confidence. He even came to auditions with me and certainly got me the part in *Godspell*. I wowed them on the *Godspell* audition. I mean *we* wowed them. We really did. I performed a musical number, one that I always love doing. It's an old music hall song by Gus Elen called 'If It Wasn't For The 'Ouses In Between':

'Oh it really is a wery pretty garden
And Chingford to the eastward could be seen;
Wiv a ladder and some glasses
You could see to 'Ackney Marshes
If it wasn't for the 'ouses in between...'

John-Michael Tebelak, who was auditioning *Godspell*, absolutely adored the song. I also did a big rock number, probably from *Grease,* only Chuck gave it 'big time'. We just stormed it and they offered me the part there and then. They actually stood up and said, "Can you do it?" I went, "What?" because that just didn't happen. You usually went away for a week or two before you knew the verdict.

The whole production of *Godspell* was huge. It was the biggest show in London and they paid me £150 a week. In 1972! Still, they were probably saving themselves a fortune having previously shelled out for David Essex.

It was meeting David on the set of *That'll Be the Day* that first got me thinking about *Godspell*. He was the one who suggested that I audition for the lead part in the West End because he was leaving. David was a massive star at that time. On the night that I took over from him at the Wyndhams Theatre, it was announced to the David Essex groupies in the audience that their hero wouldn't be appearing. The news wasn't well received. I was in my dressing room waiting to go on for my first big West End appearance and all I could hear were these screams, "David... David." He was a major teen idol and they were his adoring fans. I stepped out on stage as Jesus to a chorus of chants for David and boos for me. Some people even walked out when they realised David wasn't going to be making an appearance.

The original plan on *Godspell* was for me and another actor, Barry Stokes, to alternate the parts of Jesus and John the Baptist. We did that for about six months and then people got fed up with it: the cast got fed up with it and so did Barry and I. In the first week I played Jesus; in the second week I was John the Baptist, whose first entrance is with a bucket and sponge, used to baptise the whole cast. The auditorium was packed, the audience and cast nervous with anticipation. My first entrance was through the auditorium from the back of the stalls. You're waiting for the spotlight to hit you and the audience gasps when it does. In my hand I had a shofar, a Jewish symbolic ram's-horn trumpet. I was supposed to give a toot on the horn, which then gives the band the note for the opening number: 'Pre...pare... ye... the way' or, as David Essex sang it (and the style we had to follow), 'Pre...pare... ye... the whyyee... of the Lord...' That's the way it was sung – 'whyyee...'

Just as I was about to blow the note, a woman with a child tapped me on the shoulder and politely asked: "Could you tell me where seats M14 and 15 are?"

Taken by surprise, I just couldn't get a note out of the ram's horn. Finally, I managed to squeeze a really high squeak out of it, but it was far too high a note for me to sing from. No one could get there in fact. 'Peeeeep...'

I could see my mate in the cast, Tina Martin, crying with laughter because she just couldn't sing any higher; couldn't sing at all in fact. Awful. So neither of my two opening nights in *Godspell* – one as Jesus, one as John the Baptist – was an unqualified success.

Before I got the *Godspell* role, having suffered the *Grease* rejection and others, I did get some minor parts from auditions – small cameos in plays, a play for ITV and things at Elstree like *General Hospital*. Who remembers that? I played an electrician – a few lines here and there. I also did a play called *Beneath the Tide*. All of these are listed in the back of a blue book of mine in which I wrote down, systematically, everything – whatever it was – that I did, together with each director's name.

My time in *Godspell* was a very 'glam' period for me. I was driving in and out of central London, had a string of girlfriends and was enjoying the city and life to the full. It was certainly a more glamorous way of life than I had been used to. At the stage door of the theatre I was approached by Vanessa Redgrave – which seemed hugely glam in itself – to join the WRP (Workers Revolutionary Party). At that time, Vanessa was meeting young actors and talking to them about the state of the British theatre, the state of British politics and so on and so forth. Of course, people like me were completely star-struck. There she was, Vanessa Redgrave, six-foot-two of 'acting dynasty' wanting to talk to me. I was completely mesmerised. Naturally, it ended up with her and the WRP ringing me up in my flat in East Putney, trying to get me involved in its 'manoeuvres', which I just found a joke because they were so out of touch with what I knew working-class people to be.

The WRP would go to places like working men's clubs in the Midlands, via someone like me, all dressed in the kind of 'combat' gear that Wolfie Smith would later wear with berets and the like. However, to people in working-class communities at that time (the early 1970s), when you went out on Saturday night you dressed up. You put on your three-piece suit, polished your boots and went out with the wife on your arm. Of course, when these 'commandos' turned up, these middle-class commandos, the people in the clubs just thought they were completely insane. So, my flirtation with the WRP was brief. Thankfully I got wise and didn't get sucked in too far.

Working-class people are often falsely assumed to be left wing. Often they aren't at all; in fact, they can be very right wing. Even more often they don't know what they are. They think they ought to be left wing as a kind of birthright, but they feel and act right wing. Certainly the working-class community I grew up in had middle-class aspirations. Look what happened to the Labour party. In my case, because of my background and my failure at the eleven-plus, I was always so focused on striving for success that I couldn't believe that anyone who came from similar circumstances could be flippant or cavalier about their work. I was certainly an ambitious young guy, determined to be taken seriously and to go all the way up in his chosen profession, and that's what I had always had – a clear objective in life. That's where I was coming from.

When I was cast as Wolfie in the sitcom *Citizen Smith* a couple of years later, for a time I think I believed I *was* Wolfie Smith – the working-class crusader. I was dressing like him: I had the torn jeans and the 'Freedom for Tooting' t-shirt. I was smoking marijuana. It was as if that method-acting thing had taken over my life. That was partly why I had to drop out of it after three series because I knew I couldn't carry on playing the role; I felt as though I was starting to lose my own identity, whatever that was at the time.

EIGHT

EVERYTHING GOES TO POT

DURING THE *Godspell* period, not long after my stint at the Belgrade Theatre in Coventry, John Dicks, Tony Allen and I moved from the Hampstead apartment to a flat in East Putney and it was there that I met my first wife, Cheryl Hall.

After a whirlwind romance, I ended up getting married at the age of twenty-four. Looking back, I can't fix in my mind who or what I was then. I certainly didn't know at the time. I suppose I thought marriage would bring some sense of stability to my life. Acting can be a desperately insecure profession, particularly when you're young, so when you find security you cling on to it. There I was, this ordinary working-class lad, suddenly mixing with rock stars, aristocrats, public school boys, gays and lesbians – worlds that I had no real concept of but with which I was colliding. In that sense the stage is a great melting pot, but it can leave you rather bewildered. I think a lot of young actors, like me, jump into marriage purely as a rock to cling to for comfort and security.

The wedding was a bizarre yet lavish occasion; very much of

the time and style that marked out the early Seventies. I was wearing a white suit with wide lapels and huge flared trousers, a brown shirt and Cuban heeled boots. Oh please!

My family had all been driven down by my dad, who had just passed his test. He was totally preoccupied with just getting them there in one piece but I guessed from his attitude that he didn't want to be there at all. As we walked into the church, he said, "You're making the biggest mistake of your life." I just looked at him, too upset with his comment to give any kind of reply. It was unusual for my dad to be like that. He still quotes it now, still to this very day. I can hear him saying it, under his breath.

Just as my marriage began, *Godspell* came to an end. Cheryl and I had gone off on a Jamaican honeymoon – a bit swanky I know, but I was kind of well-off then, what with earning my £150 per week! However, unbeknown to me, the cast and crew of *Godspell* had all been given their notice. Nobody had told me because they knew I was going away on my honeymoon – perhaps they didn't want to spoil the moment for me. When I came back from Jamaica, it was to the shock of imminent closure for the show and the cast saying, "Didn't we tell you?"

I almost died. I'd spent all my money on this wedding – a wedding that Dad told me not to go through with – and then returned home to find that I'd lost the biggest job I'd ever had. There I was, a married man with a mortgage. Terrifying! Married to someone who, as it turned out, didn't share my concerns about such routine issues and was less fretful about the likely consequences. We were two reckless, young and volatile people on the brink of successful careers who seemed to think marriage was the right step.

Looking back, we had fun, were growing up together and did some amazing things, but the relationship was destined to fail. I suspect it was entirely my fault, as indeed was my break-up years later with Diana Weston. Now, with a greater understanding of myself that has developed with age, my relationship with women is better than before and my self-destructive tendencies are more under control.

Luckily for me at the time, after *Godspell* folded, financial salvation was at hand in the shape of *Get Some In*, and my first starring role in a sitcom. We were living in a flat in Ham, and from there I walked across the river to Teddington Studios and an audition for a man called Michael Mills. He was a very eccentric individual who was quite well known for producing Michael Crawford's *Some Mothers Do Have 'Em*. That was his baby.

At the *Get Some In* audition he gave me the role of Jakey Smith there and then. It couldn't have come sooner: I was so hard up that I was pleading with banks and utility companies to hold off. It was a desperate situation. I was completely broke and sinking fast, with about a thousand pounds worth of debt – serious money in 1974. I owed three hundred quid to the electricity company, a similar amount to the gas board, and had an overdraft of £280.

I was over the moon to get the job, so much so in fact that when Michael Mills started trying to pull me back down to earth I didn't really pay attention. I wish I had done. "I'm just warning you before you agree to do this, to just think," he said. "I can tell you're excited Robert, but I'd just like to say something to you. By giving you this role and you accepting it, you are giving away the rest of your life. Your anonymity will be finished. You will not be your own person. Do you understand me?"

But I didn't. It was "give me the contract and I'll do it". They were paying me £250 an episode and I had signed to do fourteen. Suddenly, I was close to having some money. When they gave us our contracts on the first day of rehearsals, Brian Pettifer, David Janson and I were all knocking on the door of the accounts office at Thames Television, asking for an advance to pay off our debts. So when Michael was trying to warn me of the perils of sitcom fame, I just thought 'yeah, yeah, whatever'. I wasn't listening to him at all. All I could think about was the fact that I'd just got a job in a 'telly' series. I know now what a great thing it was to say to a young actor. Quite touching, actually.

I was ready for the role of Jakey Smith, the Teddy boy who gets called up for National Service in the RAF in 1955; he's got no time for authority but he's not a bad lad – so no typecasting there then! Finally I'd got the Teddy boy, the role that eluded me in *That'll Be the Day*. At last I was playing the cool guy in the frockcoat and drainpipes, the beetle crushers, the fag – the whole thing. I really got into the role, helped in no small measure by a sizeable Teddy boy wig. I even improvised my first line as I walked up to the airbase gates with my suitcase in the opening scene. The guard says: "Name?"

I go: "Smif."

"Is that one 'f' or two?"

And I ad-libbed: "Fffree!"

I started what was a very happy period in my life, despite the ill-fated marriage. A year and a half of doing the series with a great bunch of people. I loved the boys in it. We all got on really well, the five of us: Brian Pettifer, David Janson, Tony Selby, Gerard Ryder and me. We also did a summer season of the show in Torquay, and that was the summer that Cheryl and I realised the same thing – that we were very different people.

How did I feel about the eventual end of the marriage? A mixture of relief that it was over but also huge disillusionment. How come my parents could be happily married for all those years and yet I couldn't even manage more than a few?

Prophetic though my dad had been, Cheryl and I did, for a while at least, have a good time. A relationship may be over, but the memories don't fade away completely. We had many showbiz friends, we travelled together, but perhaps we made the big mistake of working together too (in the film *Three For All* and *Citizen Smith*) and that, for me at least, was the final straw. But, contrary to Dad's prediction, the marriage wasn't a mistake and I don't regret it. How can I regret the adventures we shared?

On one truly memorable trip to Sri Lanka, the famous actor Vijaya Kumaranatunga (who we had been introduced to by my RADA friend Leigh Lawson) took us to Sigiriya (Lion's Rock) – a magical place overlooking the jungle – and to the Temple of the Tooth in Kandy. The monks were so overawed by Vijaya's presence that they let us into the inner sanctuary, something that tourists are never allowed to see. It was through him that we met Mrs Bandaranaika, the first woman prime minister in the world, who was the mother of his wife Chandrika (herself destined to become the country's first female president in 1994). We dined with Mrs Bandaranaika – a very friendly yet formidable woman – a number of times and it was during one of these occasions that she told us about the fatal shooting of her husband. A monk had walked into the very dining room where we were seated, pointed a loaded gun at her husband's head and shot him. Vijaya was also very politically motivated and, tragically, this led to him too being assassinated outside his own home in 1988. He always cut a majestic figure in his white sarong – and I understand that a statue of him now stands in Colombo – but I will remember him as a good friend who introduced me to the art of the Bollywood film and had a passion for Barry White!

And I can't regret working with Cheryl on the movie *Three for All*. It was directed by Martin Campbell (of Bond movie fame) and produced by Dick James (who had run Northern Songs for The Beatles before annoying them by selling out to Associated Television rather than to them). In the film I was a drummer in the band Billy Beethoven, with Graham Bonnet, Paul Nicholas and Chris Neil as the other members. Despite the aspirations of Dick James, it was obvious (even to the studio audience during the filming) that the band was going nowhere – and neither was the film. But I got to work with John le Mesurier, Richard Beckinsale and the amazing Diana Dors, a wonderfully down-to-earth yet high-living woman who mothered everyone on set.

Dad had realised that the marriage might not work at the start, so why hadn't I? It was almost as if I'd been living in a haze that finally started to clear, like I was emerging from some kind of 'Stoned' Age. Maybe Alan Bleasdale was right – the Sixties really didn't start until the Seventies! That whole period, surrounded by people who constantly smoked dope, who were puffing away on it like other people did on cigarettes, just took me away from where I wanted to go.

Perhaps inevitably, I got 'done' by the police towards the end of our relationship. Our home was always full of joints. It was unavoidable with our circle of friends, who all seemed to smoke marijuana and who all seemed to be round at our place most of the time. That's what people did in the Seventies I guess – or at least the crowd we knew. One day I was at home hoovering (yes, really!). I think I even had a pinny on. I stupidly decided to have the remains of a joint that was lying around. As I went to light it there was a knock on the front door, which I opened to an oversized group of coppers standing on the step. And me in my pinny!

"Yeah?" I said innocently, calling on every ounce of RADA training, but they ignored me and came bursting in with sniffer dogs. I didn't know it but there was a cannabis plant in the back garden. An ex-copper who was working nearby had seen it and reported it to the police, which had led to the house call. The police at the door had all seen me on the TV, so they knew who I was. As I was on the telly I just knew they'd really go for me. And why not I suppose? They went through everything in the house. Apart from the plant itself, it was all quite innocent. Anyway, I was charged and they took the plant away. Fortunately, *I* wasn't taken away!

When the court case came up it was under my real name of Stevenson, not Robert Lindsay, so I didn't get the full media attention. However, I remembered my dad's words at the wedding and I just knew I was on a path that I didn't want to be on. I didn't want to get involved with that whole scene, especially when the press lot turned up after the court case. One leading showbiz journalist, who I still see every so often, turned up at my door and stood there with a smirk on his face. "It's been brought to my attention that you have..." he said. I panicked and rang my agent who managed to stop the article somehow. But it was a real moment of catharsis – I thought, 'No, I want out of all this.'

After two series of *Get Some In* I dropped out of the show

and Karl Howman, who had been in *That'll Be the Day* with me and who shares my birthday (13 December), took over my role as Jakey Smith.

I moved on to *Citizen Smith*, another sitcom. The writer John Sullivan had seen me in *Get Some In* and so I was brought in to discuss the new project. I met with Dennis Main-Wilson, one of the show's producers and a great TV figure. Dennis had major issues with drink but was a lovely man. He always liked to boast about his reputation. He laid it on thick about Tony Hancock and how he'd 'made' him. Listening to Dennis speak, you'd think he'd made everyone from Eric Sykes to Harry Worth. You name them, he'd made them. And so Dennis was going to 'make' me the next BBC star.

NINE

OI, WOLFIE!

THURSDAY EVENING was considered a good slot for *Citizen Smith*. It went out at half past eight, straight after *Top of the Pops*, so it had a big follow-on audience. I played Wolfie Smith, Tooting's answer to Che Guevara; a loveable if somewhat lazy idealist who spends his time cooking up half-baked revolutionary schemes. The public loved him; they loved the whole show – by its peak we were getting more than twenty million viewers a week. I know there were only three TV channels back then, but even so, they were big numbers. I was getting a few hundred pounds per episode, which was alright for the time.

It all began with a pilot show, after which I met the writer, John Sullivan. He'd been a scene-shifter at the BBC who'd given Dennis Main-Wilson a script, and Dennis had bent the right ears at the BBC and helped turn it into *Citizen Smith*. John and I had this absolute, immediate rapport. We became really good pals. He was a real 'sarf' London boy, he lived in Mitcham and, at the time, I lived in Raynes Park. We used to meet 'in the middle' and play football in the park or talk about

John Lennon and our other heroes. I used to think 'this is perfect'; I didn't find that kind of bond with a writer again until I worked with Alan Bleasdale.

John went on to write *Only Fools and Horses*, and of course you all know about that. In fact one of the episodes in *Citizen Smith* was called 'Only Fools and Horses' and, if you think about it, the characters *are* pure Del Boy and co; I mean Wolfie *is* a Del Boy, Ken *is* a Rodney. The characters are all there, all from the south London area.

Citizen Smith was a fabulous series to work on and I thought that the idea of the Tooting Popular Front was great. We stole tanks and went on manoeuvres, or took part in elections and kidnapped the Conservative MP who then turned out to be the local 'mafia' boss.

There was a scene in one episode which always sticks in my mind, when Ken and I find a fingernail in a meat pie. Ken says, "Take it back. Take it back," so I go over to the bar and say, "Excuse me, I just found this in one of your meat pies." The barman just says, "Oh yeah! I'll tell you what... I'll put it there and if it's not claimed in two weeks, it's yours!" What a great line. In another episode, Wolfie says that if he ran the country, which he knew he was going to at some point, then he wouldn't have names, he'd just have numbers. Shirley, Wolfie's girlfriend, says, "What would you be?" "Well, I'd be Number One, wouldn't I." He was such a character, a typically wonderful John Sullivan creation.

We did a great scene on a tank driving through Streatham and Tooting. I had to be on top with my head sticking out of the turret as the tank tracked its way down Streatham High Street. Somehow, the tank driver took the wrong turning and all I could hear were the production guys saying, "Robert, bring the tank down... Robert bring the..." By then, there were loads of kids on it and we were lost in a traffic jam. Act of God? Of course it's God, it's Wolfie in Streatham. That's how he was treated.

And that's kind of how it became for me. It got to the stage where I couldn't go anywhere without being mobbed. I'd stop at a supermarket and bring the place to a standstill – on one occasion a security guard had to shepherd me to my car. Sometimes I was even chased, like the sitcom equivalent of a Bay City Roller!

It was my first experience of that kind of fame, a milder version of the kind of fame that David Essex was experiencing when I met him doing *Godspell*. However, in my case, it wasn't based on any rock 'n' roll fame, it was based on me being on TV each week and watched by so many people.

I remember being in Manchester, where I'd begun working at the Royal Exchange Theatre in between series of *Citizen Smith*, and there was a builder up on a roof who saw me and bellowed: "Wolfie. Power to the people!" That was what it was like – that was pretty much what everyone would do if they saw me. I was constantly the target of shouts and yells as people recognised me. Unfortunately, for that particular builder, his variation was that as he shouted, he fell, hit an awning and just went straight through it – slap! Somehow he landed on his feet and then, as if nothing had happened, just said to me, "Can you sign an autograph?" I think he was completely in shock. "Couldn't you have just walked across the street to get an autograph like everybody else?" I asked.

It was beginning to dawn on me that I was quite well known. An incident involving my new girlfriend, Diana Weston (who I met at the very end of *Citizen Smith*, while doing *The Three Musketeers* in Manchester), brought it all home. I ended up having an altercation with some blokes at a restaurant where Diana had taken me to meet some of her friends from a series she was doing called *Agony,* which starred Maureen Lipman. The fight was sparked by some innocent remark and only blew up because I was recognised as being on TV. One of our party said to me, "It must be awful for you."

Well, yes and no. Being picked on in restaurants wasn't much fun, but then my sudden flush of fame also landed me in some amazing (and bizarre) places. Rather late one night in 1980, toward the end of *Citizen Smith*, I was woken up by a phone call from Frances Tomelty who was, at that time, married to Sting. It was about three or four in the morning. As Diana handed me the phone, she said, "It's Sting in Brazil." "Oh yeah! Right!" I mumbled, thinking it was a hoax. But, sure enough, there he was on the phone. Apparently he was coming to Tooting with his band, The Police, when he returned from Brazil and wanted to know if I would introduce the concert. What else could I do but accept?

Mike Grady, my friend and *Citizen Smith* buddy (he played Ken), and I 'hosted' the gig in front of fifteen thousand fans in a big top on Tooting Bec Common. It was an extraordinary night. They even had Tommy Cooper come on and tell a few jokes in the middle of the gig.

First of all, Mike and I came on and started with a great gag. The noise was unbelievable; the crowd were screaming so much that my initial announcement was drowned out, so I ended up shouting into the microphone, "Ladies and gentlemen, the police..." And the place just went wild. The tent almost lifted off its guy ropes. We waited for what seemed like ten minutes. Because nothing happened and I just stood there, it eventually quietened down enough for me to continue, "…have asked if the owner of car registration KX2 729 could come and move it as soon as possible!" It brought the house down. Sting was there with a beanie hat on, running on and off the stage disguised as a roadie going, "F***ing brilliant, keep it up, keep going. It's brilliant. Do some more."

By now the audience were loving us, waving matches and lighters in the air and chanting "Wolfie, Wolfie…" We're thinking, 'We've got 'em here but what do we do next?' Mike said to me, "Let's do the song," and so we went into a whole Dylan-style thing on two guitars, singing:

"There's a wind just blowing through the country… hurricane of liberty… can you feel the power… can you feel the strength… can you hear the wind in me?
Don't believe the politicians… don't believe the publicity apes… they're wrong… they'll con you… say you're doing OK… shave the hairs off your gooseberries and tell you they're grapes."

Sting kept saying, "Go on… keep going!" but then I went, "Ladies and gentlemen… Sting!" and pulled his hat off as he passed by. And the place went crazy.

It was a charity gig but Mike and I had been told that we'd get some expenses. Mike had all kinds of money worries with a family of three kids and a big mortgage to pay. I'd said to Sting that we'd do the gig, but that I'd have to make sure that Mike got paid something, and I'm sure he'd said that was fine. After we'd left the stage, and Sting was up there singing 'Walking on the Moon', Mike said, "Where's our money?" "I don't know," I replied, looking around in vain for a likely someone to ask. It had all been word of mouth; it wasn't as if agents had been involved and paperwork drawn up.

Backstage, Tommy Cooper was sitting next to me. "They can't even get me a cab," he was saying, as only he could. "They tell me that they've just rung up for one and asked 'could you come to Tooting Common to pick up Tommy Cooper' and been told to 'f*** off' and had the phone put down on them."

At that point, I told Mike that I'd go and find the money. I was asking random people, "Who's in charge of this gig?" as I walked through an area full of trailers and caravans. Someone directed me to a particular trailer. I walked up the steps and, looking around, it seemed to be full of big blokes counting wodges and wodges of cash. I stood there and coughed. The main man looked up: "Yeah?"

As confidently as I could, I looked him in the eye and said: "Sting said we've got some money coming to each of us."

Impassively he answered: "Why? It's a charity evening."

"Yeah, I know, but we're getting expenses," I said diffidently.

To my relief he just said: "Oh yeah!" and gave me the cash just like that!

It was at that gig, with me turning up *as* Citizen Smith, that I realised how big it all was. The instant I appeared the place went wild. After the show a friend of mine, who'd been in the audience, commented – and still says – that the moment I walked on stage that night he'd thought, 'My God! He really is famous!'

Perhaps the most difficult thing about *Citizen Smith*, harder to deal with than suddenly being recognised everywhere I went, was the way it got caught up in my marriage break-up. Cheryl was actually in the show, playing my girlfriend, Shirley. That was a nightmare. It led to all sorts of dramas being played out on the set in front of the cast and crew. It was excruciating. It was a relief when she left, probably written out with her blessing I think.

The working environment was weird enough as it was, without the added complication of a married couple in meltdown. Sitcom was a strange world back then. You'd get in at ten, work furiously – 'block it' as we used to say – and then go to the pub or the Light Entertainment bar at lunchtime. And that was it for the day – work over. The whole daytime drinking thing worried me. It seemed like almost everyone I met on the sitcom circuit was an alcoholic. They were all drinking in the bar from half past twelve and I just found that very depressing.

'Oh God! Please get me out of this,' I'd think. That was really what frightened me off the sitcom world for twenty years after *Citizen Smith*. Everyone drank. It was the trap that so many fell into, including some of my illustrious contemporaries. At least one or two of them are no longer with us, I think as a direct result of all that.

Some of it was down to the fact that there was nothing to do. Two hours in the morning, that's all, until Thursday – the day for the studio recording. On Thursdays, you'd go in at ten o'clock and rehearse, record, rehearse, record, rehearse... until the studio audience came in the evening and you did the whole show live. It was so different from how it is now. On *My Family* we spend hours and hours in the studio and sometimes forget the studio audience altogether. In truth, it's that brief period with the audience – still usually on a Thursday – that keeps the sitcom stuff interesting for me. It's the 'live' element that I've always loved most about the process. I love the buzz of preparing, getting the show ready and then putting it on in front of an audience. I know it's a fairly easy ride because they're getting in free, will probably be big fans of the show anyway and haven't come to be critical, but even so, it's my favourite part of sitcom.

If I'm being really, really honest though, I've always seen sitcoms as a way of making a living. They are relatively cheap – but not easy – to make and, within the business, there's also this perception that they're 'cheap' intellectually. Critics often don't understand them and forget they are meant for family viewing – with all the limitations of pre-watershed scheduling. You also get the problems of inconsistency and then the actors have to work harder to compensate. It is inevitable in *any* long-running series that there will be one or two weaker scripts. Writers have the unenviable task of trying to keep standards up and it is a tribute to them that series like *My Family* please audiences of millions week in, week out.

Working on sitcoms can also be frustrating because of the quick turnaround. Bang! You have to get it absolutely right, because the moment's gone straight away. It has to be right too for the studio audience, although you have to be careful that the audience presence doesn't start to govern your performance. You have to remember that the performance isn't solely for the immediate audience – you can't make it too 'big', too theatrical. Some actors are alive to that danger, and that's probably why some choose not to play it in front of a studio audience. They play it purely for the camera so that they are not distracted.

Not only have you got to master your lines in front of a studio audience, which can be tricky sometimes, but you also have to cope with sudden applause right in the middle of a speech. It's easier to handle on stage because the 'space' is yours, but when you've got six cameras around you and microphone booms and you've been told that you've got to move from here to there, and then, right in the middle of it, there's a huge round of applause… well, it isn't as easy at it looks! I know that Zoë Wanamaker, my co-star on *My Family*, finds studio audiences a bit of a nightmare for all these reasons.

You are, in effect, a servant of two masters. I mean it's a double concept, isn't it? It's a performance for camera *and* it's a stage performance for the studio audience. *Citizen Smith* felt a bit like Variety in that respect, and I think that's one of the reasons why I decided to leave the show.

Having said all that, I did really enjoy playing Wolfie and was sad to let him go. Working with John Sullivan was enjoyable and rewarding, although he was shocked when I dropped out just as *Citizen Smith* was getting big. Going into the fourth series, it had really captured the public's imagination and the fan base was incredible. If I'd carried on with *Citizen Smith* I would have been getting two thousand pounds an episode, big money back in 1980.

At the back of my mind I couldn't get over the idea that *Citizen Smith* wasn't 'serious' enough, it wasn't the sort of acting that I wanted to be doing. The whole thing of being mobbed wherever I went seemed to add to that; the lack of anonymity conflicted with me wanting to be a 'proper' actor.

When I got a job at the Royal Exchange in Manchester, the duality of the work that I was doing – the serious and the sitcom – became more obvious. I used to go down to London for six-week stints on *Citizen Smith* and then back up to Manchester for the stage work. When we started getting a much younger audience at the theatre, I began to fully appreciate the power of television. The Royal Exchange said they'd never had so many kids coming to see shows. There were queues to see my first production, a musical called *Leaping Ginger*. I even did *The Lower Depths*, a heavy Gorky play, and there was a queue of kids around the block trying to get in, really there to see Wolfie Smith.

I wasn't offered work 'just like that' at the Exchange. I auditioned at least twice for *Leaping Ginger* and had to meet the musical director down at his flat in Islington quite a few times, and then it took them a long time to decide. By this point I'd changed agent from Marina to Felix De Wolfe, who negotiated *Citizen Smith* for me.

That wasn't the only relationship that had changed by then, of course. By the time I got to do *Leaping Ginger* up in Manchester, I was on my own and had a close relationship with my fabulous leading lady, which was not only a physical affair, but also a friendship and an emotional support. I have to confess that working opposite a very beautiful woman can have its temptations. Actors don't always have an immediate rapport, the ego is a minefield of emotions, and breaking down the barriers that exist between a leading man and a leading lady obviously makes for a better working relationship. However, once that relationship turns into an affair, then you are in trouble – it's a dangerous game to play. But when faced with the harsh realities of life, falling in love with a leading lady sometimes seems a more glamorous option – particularly when you are working on a film set in a romantic location, far away from the drudgery of domestic routine. I went through a period where I thought I was in love with my leading lady in quite a few productions. It is a terrible – but easy – trap to fall into.

Did having those affairs actually help my performances? The simple answer is no, I don't think they did. Quite the reverse in fact – it can make things very difficult. I remember Michael Elliott at the Royal Exchange saying to me: "You are a very lucky guy. A fairly handsome guy, not without talent and very likeable. You will have a lot of opportunities, but don't fall in love with your leading lady!" I was, what, twenty-three or twenty-four then and wasn't listening at all. 'It won't bother me,' I thought, but of course, he was quite right, invariably it's fatal – it can lead to all kinds of complications.

So, back to *Leaping Ginger*. It was incredibly popular. The theatre was packed out; you just couldn't get a seat to see it. I loved it. I had such a good time. I knew I'd fallen in love with the Royal Exchange. I loved the space and realised that, at last, I had found what I wanted to do. Off and on I spent the next fives years of my life there. I did *Leaping Ginger*, *Beaux Stratagem*, *Philoctetes*, *The Lower Depths*, *The Cherry Orchard* and *The Three Musketeers*, and then ended my time there with *Hamlet*, which went on to tour around the country in a tent, yes a tent, a replica of the Royal Exchange.

To stray from my theme for a moment, in true Lindsay fashion, I'm reminded of the time when Mum sent me a telegram for the opening night of *The Lower Depths,* which read "Good Luck for the Deep Cellar!" It wasn't a joke. The cast thought it was brilliant and pinned it on the noticeboard. I've still got that telegram and it makes me smile, as well as marvel that it was a time when people still sent telegrams.

I was fortunate that the people at the Royal Exchange, the directors Braham Murray and Michael Elliott in particular, realised that I was a 'proper' actor. At the same time, Braham was very aware that my telly popularity could help bring commercial success, and he used it to help push the production of *Leaping Ginger*. He had hoped that it might make it to the West End but, good though it was, the show wasn't really strong enough to go any further than it did.

It was Michael who said of me: "This man has a lot more to offer," and gave me roles like Neoptolemus in *Philoctetes* in the theatre and Edmund in *King Lear* for Granada Television. Then Braham Murray cast me as his *Hamlet* back on the stage, which turned out to be a real cathartic moment for me. It was all a chance to get out of BBC TV sitcom – a world in which I didn't feel at all comfortable, although it helped develop my acting skills in TV and comedy terms. Braham always warned that I would leave 'legit' theatre and venture into, what he called, 'cheap TV'. I wrote him a note recently: "I just wanted to let you know that most TV isn't cheap. It pays very well!"

Playing Hamlet for any actor is a revelation in that it's one of the few roles that is completely open to your own interpretation. You make the decisions; you call the shots. *Hamlet* came at a time in my career when I was beginning to swell with self-confidence and, I suspect, was the beginning of a very arrogant period. I did receive glowing reviews and the production by Braham was a huge success. For me, it was a liberation. Never once in any performance did I feel confined by the play; the role gave me such freedom and I was blessed with a cast that was prepared to accept my nightly interpretation, indeed madness. An example: during one particular performance, I found myself walking backwards, retreating from my Rosencrantz and Guildenstern to the bemused looks of the cast – they didn't know what I was doing but it made the scene electrifying. The actors were half smiling but unsure where this was going to take us. Each night was a tightrope for both actors and audience. The irony is that Hamlet is a role that can only happen once and at a certain point in your career. It's a performance that you wouldn't ever want to repeat, a part – in every sense – that embodies the title of this book.

All this took me through from 1979 to 1983, a period in which I also did a whole range of BBC Shakespeare: *Much Ado About Nothing, Twelfth Night, All's Well That Ends Well* and *A Midsummer Night's Dream*, as well as the aforementioned *King Lear* for Granada, a version that starred Laurence Olivier, the man everyone wanted to work with. Suddenly I was busy and buzzing with new projects and productions. I was enjoying life in my own apartment above Manchester's Arndale Centre (that would later be blown to smithereens by the IRA).

I don't want to overplay the Road to Damascus stuff, but I think my time at the Royal Exchange was when I 'found' myself. It was perfect. It was when I got into real 'heavyweight' theatre, doing the classics both on stage and on television. It was an area of acting that I'd neglected because of my rather whacky marriage and the seemingly urgent need for money. Fortunately, once I'd done all this work at the Royal Exchange, things were beginning to change and evolve. I was being offered serious stuff and, of course, *Citizen Smith* was still going strong.

I thrived on being busy, on being in work. And I was thankful to have that work, I always have been. When I went for a careers advice session at school I can remember the master saying, "Of course, as an actor you will never, ever be constantly in work – you do realise that don't you?" "Well it's a risk I'm prepared to take," I said, in the typically foolhardy teenage way. And it's paid off – I've never stopped. Thinking about it now, it seems slightly ironic that I came from a mining town whose fortunes have gone down and down, a place where all the industries (the very industries that the careers advice suggested we enter) are closed and where people have struggled to find work or to keep their jobs. I got out and got lucky – I've been in a business where I've never stopped working.

I don't think I ever really got my hands dirty in a theatrical sense until I started working at the Royal Exchange. I am not sure that's the right way to put it, but it's a workman's phrase isn't it? Prior to that I suppose I'd been a bit 'fluffy', I'd winged it all the way through, but then for the first time I just thought no, I'm going to get hands-on here and start doing something worthwhile.

It was crucial in my decision to quit *Citizen Smith*. The Royal Exchange reminded me of why I came into acting. It wasn't about celebrity and it wasn't about making money. It was about, genuinely about, communication and the fact that I had a talent for it. Of course, leaving the sitcom wasn't an easy decision – it felt like the pressures on me at that point were huge. I was being offered everything! There I was, a twenty-two-year-old actor suddenly making the big time. At that time in the 'young' TV comedy category there were only two of us: Richard Beckinsale and me – that was it really.

The BBC tried to put some pressure on me to stay and do another series and so did John Sullivan, so it might seem like it was a bold decision to leave, but actually it wasn't. It didn't seem brave at the time. I'd broken up with Cheryl. I'd got rid of the mortgage. We'd sold the house and split the proceeds and, therefore, I was back to what I should have been in the first place –

a single man without any responsibilities who could actually do whatever he fancied doing.

TEN

GOING LEGIT

I WAS offered all sorts of other TV after *Citizen Smith* but decided I was off to the Royal Exchange in Manchester to do the serious stuff. I was really getting into the theatre work by then, and had also begun travelling down to London to do the Shakespeare play cycle for BBC1. It was great to be meeting and working with people like Jonathan Miller and Elijah Moshinsky, the director, with whom I was to develop a very successful if somewhat strained relationship.

As I've mentioned, I struggled with the duality of being an entertainer and an actor: which side would come out on top? I had this sense that I was being 'split'. Despite the light entertainment froth, there was another side of me that was very, very determined to become a 'serious' actor.

Perhaps there's a certain snobbishness there, a certain disdain for light entertainment which, I suspect, was passed down to me from my mother. She didn't like the celebrity side of my life at all. She didn't like the fact that I was chased in the street and asked for autographs; she thought I was above all that. Mum encouraged me to get away from light entertainment and into theatre. I think she felt that some of the television work I was doing was rather vulgar, to use an old-fashioned term. In some ways her attitude reflected her background. It wasn't that she'd always been used to something better, quite the opposite in fact, it was that light entertainment represented everything that she wanted to move on from.

She'd always had aspirations for me. She was impressed by RADA, by the Royal Exchange and Shakespeare. When I did things like that she felt that I was doing something that I should be doing and something that I was good at.

When I was doing *The Entertainer* years later, I modelled my Archie Rice on an entertainer that we, as a family, used to see at the miners' holiday camp we went to every summer. Dad wasn't a miner himself, but we lived in a mining community and he knew miners at his local working man's club, and that must have been why we got invited along. It was basically a poor man's Butlins. In fact, the genuine Butlins was right next door, visible from our chalet through the barbed wire fence. Over on their side they had a really pristine beach and a funfair, and I'd sit there thinking, 'One day we'll go to Butlins.' It was as if I thought that was where the rich people went!

Actually, our side wasn't so bad. We had a roller-skating rink, a bowling alley and an outdoor swimming pool that was more like a public lido with communal showers – so that was something of a home from home for the miners!

The entertainer in question was a lovely performer. His evening stuff was probably a bit crude, but the special children's shows he did were just funny. I remember my sister won a competition in one of his shows, as she looked like Shirley Temple with the ringlets. At night, my cousin Des and I used to follow him around and he'd always be a bit legless, having finished his shows for the night. He would greet us with, "Alright lads! Eh? Alright? Great!"

He stuck in my mind but he stuck in my mum's as well, helping to shape her opinions on what she considered to be low-life Variety entertainers. They were always rather a seedy, drunken, end-of-the-pier lot. To her, people who did Shakespeare or went to RADA didn't do that sort of thing. God knows what my mum would have thought of my actual performance as Archie Rice playing *The Entertainer* – playing the person she probably never wanted me to be.

She loved it when I spoke properly and showed off the fact that I could speak in that way, that my accent had changed and that I was suddenly speaking 'the way I am speaking now' in a pub in Ilkeston. "He went to RADA for that, you know," she would proudly proclaim.

When I was playing Wolfie with all his "Yeah! Alright! Power to the People" stuff, it was much too close to where we all came from. She didn't like me playing that type of role and she didn't like me doing kitchen-sink drama either. Kitchen-sink land, as rendered tangible by John Osborne, was where we lived and the people we knew.

As I have said, my mum's side of the family came from travellers and it was a world she wanted to move as far away from as possible. Getting into the *Royal* Academy for Dramatic Art and, of course, going to the *Royal* Exchange and the *Royal* Shakespeare Company, everything that was 'touched by royalty' had appeal for her. In short, she wanted 'class'. Little wonder then that there's that ambivalence in me of being part entertainer, part 'legitimate' actor.

I'm often struck by that funny word 'legitimate', as in 'legit-imate theatre'. In *The Entertainer,* Archie's got that line: "I'd gone legit for a while just then, and I'd been in *The Tale of Two Cities.*" In this old sense, legit theatre relates to plays acted by professional actors, rather than revues, music hall or some forms of musical comedy. Indeed, anything else was therefore consid-ered illegitimate, and the wrong side of the tracks from my mum's perspective. Of course, hers wasn't an isolated opinion. Even today I know actors who've been in the RSC for years who have a real hatred for people who are 'well known', who've made it through TV.

They probably reflect a more general attitude towards the acting profession. Do the public see it as a 'proper' job? Do they respect it? Do I? Truthfully, I don't think I've ever really respected or trusted the profession. My schooling laid the foundations for suspicion, with maths and English teachers stressing that acting wasn't a serious job. The strange characters that I met in the amateur dra-matic world didn't exactly scream 'respect'. They were all very eccentric, with all the campery and pseudo-intellectualism that seemed to go with 'am-dram'. I think I've always been a bit removed from the profession in that sense, perhaps frightened of letting myself go. That's why I'm not a 'luvvie' and never could be.

Every so often I glimpse the 'outsider's' perspective on the acting world, and the low level of respect it commands. When I was doing *Me and My Girl* at the Adelphi Theatre, the director Mike Ockrent came up to me after one performance and said he'd just been entertaining Princess Margaret in the theatre bar. Apparently, she'd said: "Where did you get that leading man from? A circus?" Great, thanks for the royal seal of disapproval. On another occasion I'd gone to Parliament to lobby for Equity, which had got us involved in some campaign or other. I remember speaking to a well-known Labour minister at the inevitable photo session. "Oh, that's what we need actors for," he said. "So we can get photographed with them."

Perhaps I'm as guilty as anybody. I've always wanted respect for my acting, but when that respect has come, occasionally I've turned round and kicked it in the face. It's almost as if I have no respect for the *me* that is the actor. That's a difficult one to deal with because I've always admired figures like Laurence Olivier, actors who take themselves seriously, take their profession seriously and who have a total commitment to it, come what may. But there's so much of me that wants so many other things. I need to have the family life, the money and the adoration as well as respect. Sometimes I'm rather flippant about my profession and about *me* and that's probably why I've ended up doing so much comedy. Comedy is always my escape route, my get-out clause to avoid having to take *me* seriously!

My wife Rosie has observed that at some point in the course of a role, whatever I'm doing, I'll start to hate it. She says she can count on it. "I knew you'd start hating *The Entertainer*," she told me. "It doesn't matter how big it is, or that everyone is seeing it and it's getting the best reviews, at some point you'll begin to hate it."

She's right. And I've realised that it comes down to that snobbishness passed on from my mother. It's almost like a self-disgust, a self-loathing about my life in a profession that I think, at the extreme, can be cheap and tarty – or 'vulgar' and 'seedy' to quote my mum. When it's popular culture, designed for the masses, it can be a bit downmarket – as Noel Coward said, "Strange, the potency of cheap music." And so there are times when I don't really respect the profession. However, I don't draw quite the same boundaries that Mum did. To me, it's all about entertaining, whether you are King Lear or Ken Dodd. What's the difference? When you see the likes of Sir Ian McKellen doing Widow Twankey in panto or popping up in *Coronation Street*, the different grades of acting blur into that amorphous catch-all, entertainment. And, I'm afraid, to some people in my world, that means 'cheap'.

When I meet successful business people, I sometimes think, 'Why aren't I doing something proper like them?' It's as if entertaining on stage every night isn't a proper occupation, as if it's too frivolous. I can't tell you what it feels like sometimes on a hot summer's day, driving into the West End of London, watching everyone sitting in cafes or walking along by the river and you know that you are going in to do two shows. Two shows! For what?

It can be terrible when you start picking on yourself in that way and your self-esteem plummets. In truth, playing Archie Rice was fine because there's that bitterness in the role, but if you're doing something like Bill Snibson in *Me and My Girl*, which is meant to be all fun, then it's hard work. At least with Archie you can go with the feelings of the character. The director of *The Entertainer* said to me: "If you hate it, bring it on stage. If you hate the audience, let them see it." Because, of course, that's what the play is all about.

The move from *Citizen Smith* to the Royal Exchange was all part of this search for credibility and, I suppose, subconsciously, to fulfil my mother's aspirations for me. After I went for the *Leaping Ginger* audition, and was waiting for a decision to materialise, I went off to Morocco with Cheryl, driving to Marrakech in my Renault.

It was a fairly bizarre trip, the main event of which was the car being 'emptied' by thieves in Tangiers. They even took the seats. I had to drive a husk of a car onto the return ferry. It had a patched up steering wheel and the gearshift knob had been replaced with a lump of wood. I sat on a box. I drove up to get on the boat in Tangiers and the customs guy just stood there looking at me aghast. What a sight! They were smelling my car for marijuana – not the dogs, the men! They thought I was a complete airhead.

We got into more than one scrape on that holiday. On one day we were picked up in Marrakech and taken up to somewhere in the Atlas Mountains to do a 'deal' with a Berber. The guide directed us with me driving along in the Renault. You have to remember that this was back in the early 1980s, when Morocco had a real 'Third World' feel. Being taken up to a remote village was quite something; it wasn't really on the average tourist's itinerary. The Berbers all came out to look at us. At first they all just thought, 'blonde girl – hooker'! They started prodding and touching Cheryl, trying to do deals for *her*.

Just as I was thinking, 'Let's get out of here, this is terrifying,' they gave us a joint to share with them. I could see a gang of kids actually walking on the car and, while we smoked, I tried to plan a quick getaway. We were taken down to a hut and offered mint tea. Looking around, I suddenly realised that there were no other women there, just twenty guys – and all of them staring at Cheryl.

"We'd better go. We've got to get back to the hotel," I whispered. The next thing I saw was a hand on Cheryl's knee. Maybe I was being over-dramatic, but I knew we had to get out of there straight away so we fled. I recently returned to Marrakech and what a change – Berbers on bikes with baseball hats and mobile phones!

Throughout the Moroccan trip, which lasted about a month and a half, I was desperate to hear whether I had actually got the part in *Leaping Ginger*. Every time I managed to find a phone box (remember there were no mobile phones back then), I was ringing the Royal Exchange. Cheryl got bored of me making calls every day and became angry. To her it was 'just a job' so why get so agitated about it. She couldn't work out what was so important. I knew that it was more than that for me – for me it was a change of life. I could see how different our attitudes to work and life were. Eventually I got the news that I'd been waiting for – I'd got the part and couldn't wait to get back to England.

The moment I went to the Royal Exchange, the day I drove up there, having packed my bags and left our home, I knew that it was the end of the marriage and that I really wouldn't see Cheryl again. It was a huge moment. I also felt a sense of freedom, of doing what I wanted to do.

Not all of the stage work was happening at the Royal Exchange. During this period I also appeared in a production of *The Changeling*, directed by Peter Gill at the Riverside Studios in Hammersmith. It was an intense period of rehearsals, almost ten weeks, for this one show. Brian Cox played the lead and David Troughton was also in it, both wonderful, wonderful actors. When I started doing that production I suddenly realised that this was the real me. It was a great feeling, a wonderful discovery and a revelation to myself that I loved it so much.

The popular TV work did impact on my move into serious stuff. The stage work was deeply satisfying but by this point, I was, whether I liked it or not, a celebrity. As the most well-known person in *The Changeling*, people were coming to see me and, of course, I realised that was the power of television.

Continuing my acting 'change', I then did six Shakespeares for the BBC: two, I think, produced by Cedric Messina, who started the whole epic BBC Television Shakespeare series in the 1970s, and then the rest produced by Jonathan Miller who took over running the cycle. This was just as well as the Messina plays were nicknamed 'the creaky floorboard productions' and Jonathan Miller transformed them into more vital and immediate productions with better camerawork – particularly on the soliloquies.

The first one I did was *Twelfth Night* with Felicity Kendal, Sinead Cusack, Robert Hardy, Alec McCowen and Trevor Peacock – a great cast. Then it was *All's Well That Ends Well*, followed by *Cymbeline* and *A Midsummer Night's Dream* (both with Elijah Moshinsky in the director's chair), which were absolutely stunning productions, beautiful to look at and probably the best of the whole lot. Elijah had great visual flair and helped build on the classier productions introduced by Jonathan Miller.

That's when I worked with the great Helen Mirren, in *Cymbeline*. We would cycle to the Acton rehearsal rooms together – she used to call in for me on her bike as I lived in Chiswick and she lived just up the road in Parsons Green. We became good mates but, of course, like many of her leading men, I fell head over heels in love with her because I have a very vivid imagination. I thought it was reciprocated, but much to my horror I realised how wrong I was.

For one scene Helen and I ended up spending the whole day in bed together (did I mention how tough acting can be...?). It's a scene where I discover a secret about her character, having been sent over to England by her lover to test her. I tell him something about her body and he jumps to the conclusion that I've slept with her, but in fact, I haven't. I've just crawled into her bed at night having given her a drink and I've wandered around her naked body and found this mole and told him about it. He then flips and thinks that she's been unfaithful. I hope you followed that! Read it yourself – Shakespeare tells it much better!

That evening, after we'd finished the bed scene (during which I confess I had completely misinterpreted her acting and misread the signals), I gave her a lift back to her place in the car. I was thinking, 'This is it – she's taking me back.' We got some fish and chips. We stopped at the lights on Hammersmith Broadway and she banged on this guy's window in the car next to us and said, "Have you got a fag?" And this guy, somewhere between bemused and mesmerised, gave Helen a cigarette. And all the time I'm thinking, 'Yeah, I'm with Helen Mirren... I've made it big time.' Helen wasn't as well known back then, but she was – as she is now – totally revered for her acting, and of course she's always been a 'dame' in one sense or another. As you might expect, nothing went to plan as we arrived at her place. We got to her flat, she opened the door and standing there was this huge Irishman, the actor Liam Neeson. "Oh, hello Bob. Nice to meet you. Thanks for bringing her home," he said in his wonderful soft Irish accent.

It was all I could do to stammer: "Not at all, thank you very much... thank you."

Oh, poor deluded Lindsay. I had no idea Helen was seeing Liam, let alone living with him. She is so canny, she really is, but I love her dearly.

That time spent at the BBC doing the Shakespeares was very much a kind of repertory period for me, lasting, I guess, from about 1980 to 1983. After that, I went over to Granada TV and *King Lear*, in which Laurence Olivier played his last great Shakespearean role. He won an Emmy for his portrayal of the ageing King. Laurence (or Larry as everyone called him) had a big effect on my life. He wrote me many letters and actually came to see me twice in *Me and My Girl*. During filming at Granada one day we were in the canteen when the cast of *Are You Being Served?* wandered in to get lunch. Larry leaned over to me and confided: "I'd love to be in that show." Can you imagine, a legend like Olivier secretly pining for a bawdy sitcom. On another occasion we sat in my dressing room at the Adelphi Theatre after a performance of *Me and My Girl* and he said to me that one day I should do *The Entertainer*, a show (and film) he'd starred in himself. It happened eventually, in 2007, when I'd reached the right sort of age to do it.

When I was about to do *The Entertainer* all those years later, I realised that the character that I was going to play, Archie Rice, had made the same sort of journey that I had. I'd spent my time in both sitcoms and in serious theatre, and that's exactly how it is for Archie Rice: he's Variety and light entertainment, but he's trying to take his performing seriously, trying to get that credibility.

It's well known and often voiced that, as an actor, you never know where your next job is coming from – how many times have you heard an actor say that? However, it came as a bit of a shock to discover that Laurence Olivier was as insecure as the rest of us. He worried about his next job and what he was going to leave his children when he died. You might think that someone as successful as Olivier wouldn't have money and security issues like everyone else, but unless you're in the big Hollywood star bracket you don't necessarily earn big money.

Even while I was hitting my stride with the Shakespearean work, I kept adding to the lighter side of my CV as well. I did a comedy series called *Seconds Out*, playing a boxer. That was for the BBC where, technically, I was still a contract actor. I'd been given a contract when I got the *Citizen Smith* job, and was actually the last actor at the BBC to be given a contract that stretched beyond a single production. There were only a few of us at the BBC that got that kind of deal. Besides me, there were the likes of Richard Beckinsale, Penelope Keith and Ronnie Barker. That was the last time you were treated like that, like being part of a studio, as in Hollywood (yeah, dream on Lindsay!).

A contract with the BBC might sound like a meal ticket, but actually they weren't all they were cracked up to be. Before the 1980s, those contracts were virtually 'buy out' agreements, agreed and endorsed by the union, by Equity, who negotiated behind our backs and effectively sold everyone out. If, for instance, your show was a success and got a repeat run, you only got a tiny amount for the repeat – the figures certainly didn't move in line with inflation. When the video/DVD era arrived it looked like actors were going to get even less for their contribution. Thankfully, my agent was on the ball with *Citizen Smith* and got me a '50p slice'.

The whole thing looks like a crazy mess in retrospect. For example, an actor like Ronnie Barker wasn't getting paid properly for *Porridge*. He was probably getting an outright payment of two thousand pounds or so for an entire series. A man of his stature, showing on prime-time TV! The problem was that Equity, the union that was negotiating for us, that was responsible for setting up agreements on our behalf and securing our income, simply wasn't up with the times. It was full of old stagers: Variety artists, pub entertainers, trapeze artists, cabaret performers and so on; it wasn't run by people who understood how the industry was (and still is) changing.

Equity needed a man like David Puttnam to say, "Look, this is what is going to happen and we must prepare for it." They just had no concept of the way the industry was headed. They didn't put the failsafe clauses in agreements and contracts that would bring financial protection against the effects of future developments and issues. At the time I was trained, the emphasis was on the theatre. Equity didn't understand that TV was going to be the big, big thing. Film, they obviously knew about, but only in terms of general release features, not as a source of income from video or DVD.

A few years ago I went along to an Equity meeting with Denis Lawson, Zoë Wanamaker and Ken Cranham. It was suggested to Equity that they needed a Screen Actors Guild like they have in the States and that they had to get a suitable chairman, someone who was more like a businessperson and who really knew the media world. However, they didn't listen because Equity, unsurprisingly, is run by actors (some of them failed actors at that), and actors aren't businessmen, they are creative types. They needed someone on the board with the vision to say, "Listen guys, terrestrial is going to be over soon. You know we are going into satellite, cable, high definition..." Had they done so, they could have prepared their membership for the changes to come. Their failure to do so means that, in the age of More4, UK Gold and all the rest, your fee gets split all the way down until it virtually disappears. They just roll your old shows out all day on some small cable channel and you hardly get a penny. Scandalous really.

Anyway, back to my agreement at the BBC. Because I was still a contract actor after *Citizen Smith*, I thought I might be able to get myself on a BBC director's course. However, I discovered that because I hadn't been to university, they wouldn't let me take one. That really pissed me off. How ridiculous was that? I suddenly realised that directors at the BBC were all university educated, mostly at Oxford or Cambridge – and that was basically what the BBC wanted.

It wasn't my first encounter with certain outdated attitudes at good old Auntie Beeb. John Sullivan wrote a scene for *Citizen Smith* that caused a bit of a stir. It featured Ken as a pavement artist. Wolfie is out busking – making no money at all – and all the while, along the street, Ken is drawing this amazing image in chalk – a scene of the Crucifixion. People were dropping money into Ken's hat. Then, just as we're all enjoying the painting, a bird shits on it, the crowd goes "ahhh" and Ken promptly incorporates it into the scene. The bystanders go "oohh" and applaud, while an American guy offers to buy the pavement slab for, like, ten grand. I intervene with, "I'm his agent, OK," and start doing a deal for the slab. That's the scene – a very funny one indeed.

We got ready to shoot the scene, which we were filming on Acton High Street. So there I am, singing and strumming a song in my best busking style, just down the road from Ken. I walked over to Ken, as planned, and there on the pavement... is a Buddha! "Whoa! Hang on! Cut! What's this?" I said. "Oh yeah, the BBC vetoed the Crucifixion scene," replied the director. "But this spoils the whole scene, and, anyway, now you're going to upset the Buddhists," I replied. So we refused to do the scene

– this was Wolfie's first rebellion. There were memos coming out from the BBC and we realised that the man who was then running Light Entertainment was apparently a fervent Roman Catholic and had banned the pavement Crucifixion personally.

I suppose that was when things began getting a bit blurred in my mind. Who was indignant here? Robert Lindsay or Wolfie Smith? I began to feel like I was playing this working-class hero (however inept he might be) on British television but it was getting a bit mixed up with the real me, this working-class lad who was pulling in millions of viewers a week. And then, when the BBC started telling me I wasn't good enough to take this or that course... well, I suppose the chip on the shoulder grew a bit more.

ELEVEN

CONTROLLING BIG FACE

THROUGHOUT THE sitcoms and Shakespeare, I had been trying to keep my performances more subtle for TV.

I've mentioned my 'big face' before; how I had to work hard at being less expressive in front of the camera. John Esmonde and Bob Larbey, who wrote *Get Some In* (and were also behind comedies like *Please Sir!* and *The Good Life*), had always commented that, because I had this 'big face' and 'big eyes', I really, really had to calm down because it could fill up the shot too much. I did overuse my face a lot. I didn't know I was doing it, but any slight movement of my eyes would look so exaggerated. As Spike Milligan once said (not about me!), "He had a mobile face... he always took it with him." John Esmonde sent me a note once after seeing me in *Citizen Smith*: 'If you don't stop being so expressive you are going to ruin it. You are very funny, but you're overdoing it. You're such a big personality, you have such an expressive face, but you need to calm down a bit'.

I thought it was a really good note and took his advice very much to heart, but in fact it didn't really sink in until I started doing the Shakespeare cycle for the BBC, when I was working with film and TV directors like Stuart Burge and Elijah Moshinsky; people who would say, "No, no, no, just tone it down." I remember doing a *Sunday Times* commercial for Stephen Frears at that time and he told me the same thing: that I could be over-expressive.

My breakthrough in sorting out the 'big face' came when I did *Cymbeline*, when I first wore a prosthetic that made me look completely unlike me. I think that was when I realised that my strength was in character acting and not in performing through myself. Iachimo was the first role I had where I saw myself and went, "That's not me, that's not me at all. That's someone else."

That was when I found a way to create a character through artifice. My recently retired agent, Lo Hamilton, came to a screening of a TV piece in which I played Tony Blair and said that she didn't know how I did it, but I always seemed to be someone different.

Playing Tony Blair, I had special contact lenses in and a gap in my teeth and was doing the Blair hand movements. What is weird is that I don't do 'impressions' as such – I'm no Rory Bremner – but there is something inside me that helps me assume the role. Wolfie in *Citizen Smith* was very much *not* me, but it seemed so natural that people used to say, "Oh you're just playing yourself." Only I wasn't. If anything it was the other way round – Wolfie started playing me in real life. I was playing him for real because I rather liked the fact that he was cool and hip and people loved him. It was a very dangerous thing to get into.

What I've learnt is that, like many other actors, once I am in front of the cameras or on stage, I suddenly become someone else completely. That's what I have to do – I have to transform, to assume the role. I always felt that I wanted to change myself in some way, and was never totally happy in a role just looking like 'me'. Of course, what I've realised over the years is that you actually change character from within. You don't really need the false teeth, the eyes, the make-up, the humps and stuff, because you can change your body physically just by 'thinking' the character – a form of method acting I suppose. I've learnt that the external action results from internal thought. On a simple level, for example, you can see it if the character cries, and I achieve that internally, remembering something or someone that affects me enough to bring on the tears.

Julie Walters is an expert at becoming the character. Indeed, in my opinion she's the perfect English actress and has played my lover, my wife *and* my mother – without make-up! Equally, Helen Mirren has that same ability. When I worked with her, she would tease me and we'd play around in between takes, but when the camera came on, she would become someone else, she'd just change. On the other hand, I think there are also actors who seem to play themselves. They are very much 'personalities' and it is all about getting the next series developed around them.

I remember talking to Richard O'Sullivan about this once when we were at London Weekend Television and I asked him if he ever wanted to do other things. He said, "That's not what my audience expects!" I realised that wasn't something *I* wanted to do. I didn't want to be myself. I wanted to be other things. That's probably why I've tried to be versatile, I guess, and tried to be, in performance, somebody who isn't actually me, not even a 'larged-up' version of me.

Analysing and preparing for a role is important and, of course, I do the background and historical research, but there comes a point when you have to let go. It's like you have to jump off a cliff. It's the moment you jump and then, if you've got the wings, you'll fly and if you don't, you'll drop. If you've got the material and you understand it, you're suddenly flying and everything's fine and it's very exciting, but if you've not quite understood it, you plummet.

I do 'become' this other person, but it doesn't necessarily happen just like that. Usually it occurs a little way into the run of a piece, and when it does, it's *the* most extraordinary feeling; when you're at one with yourself, the character and an audience, and you are not alarmed by anything, not even by sitting on a stage in front of one or two thousand people. It's quiet and you're speaking to them and suddenly you realise that you are totally in control and you've become the character. It happened to me in *Cyrano de Bergerac*. It happened in *Becket*. It happened a couple of times in *Richard III*.

Tennessee Williams described a similar concept in *Cat on a Hot Tin Roof*, referring to it as the 'click'. The alcoholic guy in the play says he has to keep drinking until he gets the 'click', the point at which he feels like he's fine and doesn't have to drink anymore. Like a drug then, it's the moment on stage when you get 'it'. You keep working at getting 'it' and suddenly for some reason, it could be during a Wednesday matinee or a Thursday night, you actually get 'it'. You've clicked. The part and the character are yours. It's a fantastic feeling.

Some actors talk about being in a trance-like state when it happens, or say that it feels like you've gone to the 'other side', as it were. In a sense it does feel like that. I've had that 'out-of-body' experience a couple of times, but it's not quite trance-like. It's just that you suddenly feel calm. Performing, any performing, any speaking, any form of communication is stressful; it's based on adrenaline, based on the desire to make sure that you have an impact on someone. Of course, when that moment of calm comes and you're just sitting back, being the character without having to push it, it's extraordinary. It's the best drug you'll ever get.

When you're in that state – completely in character – it's impossible to 'corpse'. I've only ever corpsed on occasions when the 'click' hasn't happened. I can't imagine you would ever make Helen Mirren corpse or Frances De La Tour or Julie Walters, because they would be in their character, whereas someone who's only slightly in character, who hasn't made the big leap, could still 'go' at any moment.

Learning all the 'craft' stuff helped my work on stage in the early 1980s, building my reputation as a serious actor, but it also came in useful for the more down-to-earth stuff, not least for *Seconds Out*. That was an interesting time. I like to look back on it now as my 'fitness period'. I've certainly never been as fit as I was then, either before or since. I started training at the Acton Boys' Club and the East End's famous Thomas A' Becket with the boxers Frank Bruno and Alan Minter. In fact I sparred with Alan – sorry, pretended to spar – just before his big fight with Marvin Hagler at Wembley Arena, a fight that ended in a riot after Minter lost in three rounds.

We did twelve half-hour episodes of *Seconds Out* in all and each one was called a 'Round', as in boxing, with Round One the first week, Round Two the second week and so on. Ken Jones was in it with me, playing my trainer, and so was the gorgeous Leslie Ash who was with Rowan Atkinson at the time.

I used to lark about a lot between takes because, by then, I'd worked out that if you kept the studio audience amused by your antics off camera, you'd keep their attention when you needed it during recording. That's half the fun (and half the challenge) with a studio audience – keeping them amused and involved. I remember there was a train sequence, which we had to do with all four of us supposedly travelling somewhere. We'd stopped recording at one point and I started doing that thing of walking along the side of the carriage as if the train is still going. The audience were screaming with laughter, absolutely loving it.

Rowan came up to me afterwards and said that he wasn't keen on the sitcom, that it wasn't his kind of comedy, but that he loved the moments when I was doing all the off-camera stuff with the train. He thought those bits were far funnier than the actual sitcom.

All very flattering, but I've never been too sure how I feel about that side of me. Most actors seem to have that clown side; it seems to go with the territory. When Laurence Olivier came to see me in *Me and My Girl*, he used to say to me in that wonderful whispery voice of his: "I love all that 'business' you do. Why don't you try this?" He taught me the routine where you put a sugar lump on a spoon, hit the spoon to flick the sugar up in the air and then catch it in your cup. I couldn't believe it – one of the greatest serious actors teaching me how to clown around.

In truth, Rowan's dislike for the comedy in front of the camera on *Seconds Out* was well judged. It probably wasn't a very funny series. Perhaps you can't make a funny series about a boxer. Or maybe you can but we just didn't manage it. After all, if you can make a funny series about a dentist – like they have with *My Family* – then why not a boxer?

I felt more confident about the quality of the theatre work I was doing in that period, particularly *Hamlet* at the Royal Exchange. Directed by Braham Murray, we began with it in

Manchester and then took it on tour. Performance-wise, *Hamlet* was a bit of a milestone for me, not least because the British press seemed to start taking me seriously. I began to shake off the *Citizen Smith* albatross.

Hamlet was very important for me in another way. It was the production that David Aukin and Richard Armitage saw me in. They were a pair of producers looking for a lead, a Bill Snibson, for their new production of *Me and My Girl*. Their trip to watch *Hamlet* in Manchester began a sequence of events that would take me all the way to Broadway.

I'd worked with David Aukin when he was artistic director at Hampstead Theatre, in *How I Got That Story*, a play about a newspaper reporter in the Vietnam War. That was also when I first met Ron Cook, who would become a close friend (and, later, best man for my marriage to Rosemarie Ford). Ron basically played the whole Vietnam War – all the characters – while I was the journalist – it was only a two-man show. It was a brilliant play, but somewhat tragically we put it on during the week of Charles and Diana's wedding. I think we had one person in for the Saturday matinee, some guy who we ended up taking for a drink afterwards.

Anyway, David Aukin. He'd gone on to run the Haymarket Theatre in Leicester where he and Richard Armitage were planning to put on a revised production of *Me and My Girl*. David had told Richard: "The guy you want for *Me and My Girl* is an actor called Robert Lindsay." Richard didn't really know who I was – he remembered me vaguely from *Citizen Smith* – and so they travelled to Manchester in Richard's Rolls Royce to see me do *Hamlet*.

David Aukin thought it was one of the best Hamlets he'd

ever seen, but he would say that, wouldn't he, because he's always been a big supporter of mine. Richard, on the other hand, just couldn't understand it. "Why on earth have you brought me up here to see this actor playing Hamlet?" he'd said. "Look, there is a true clown," responded David. "The perfect clown for you to build *Me and My Girl* around." Richard wasn't convinced – in fact he gave up on *Hamlet* at the interval.

But David wouldn't let it lie. He even sent a mutual friend, Dallas Smith, to see me when I was on holiday in Ibiza, to persuade me to do the show. I was there with Diana and our friends Tommy and Cookie Vance, and Dallas turned up clutching the script of *Me and My Girl*. I threw it into the swimming pool! I thought, 'I'm a serious actor. I'm not doing this!' Dallas dutifully fished it out, dried it and, of course, I ended up doing the show. It was David who really, really pushed for me to be considered for the part, and David who convinced me that I should do it.

By this point, I'd worked out what I thought was a wonderful scheme of working: I would go down to the BBC, earn a bit of money, then go back up to the Royal Exchange and do the fulfilling stuff. So, for instance, while I was doing *Hamlet* on stage I was also appearing in *Give Us A Break*, a BBC series with Paul McGann. It was a fabulous period. I had money to live on, had my own place in Manchester and was also earning enough to buy a place in London, firstly an apartment in Maida Vale and then, after I'd met Diana, a house in Chiswick that we shared.

I'd got my acting life to the point where I was enjoying the mix a great deal, and it seemed to be working financially too. At last I felt sorted. I suppose I felt like I'd made it. Don't ask me how it all fell into place, it just did. Actually, I'm often asked how you get started in acting, how you become successful or how to choose the right parts to do well in TV, theatre or film. And the truth of it is I don't know; I don't think anyone really knows. There are no easy answers or quick solutions. Fortunately, most of my decisions have worked out for me in the end. When I was in my early twenties, it was more about getting by, because at that stage in my life I certainly didn't have anyone to fall back on. I didn't have parents that could give me money and there was no silver spoon, anywhere. Believe me, I looked! It was all about survival and wanting to be successful. I'm afraid that's why certain people in this business will walk over anyone else to get what they want.

TWELVE

DOING THE BUSINESS

MY AMERICAN adventures, which centred on Broadway and included the inevitable flirtation with Hollywood, began with *Me and My Girl*. Thank goodness I decided to take the role. It had been a close call. It started with the usual "shall I, shan't I" debate, with me initially being persuaded to do it but then deciding that actually no, I didn't want to do it, before finally going full circle and saying, "Oh, alright then, I'll do it!"

The thing is, you see, I've always been a ditherer. I've got a reputation for not making up my mind. I've even changed my mind several times about writing this book! I see nothing wrong with the 'definite maybe' approach to decision making. A lot of actors are like that with the same reputation for indecisiveness. The problem with decisions in this business is that they don't just affect the next thing you are going to be working on, they affect everything – in fact, they can affect the rest of your life. Your career can turn on a single decision. You have to make a choice about what you're going to do, when you're going to do it, where you're going to do it and how you're going to do it. I've always found that very difficult, and in many ways it's probably been my downfall. If I'd made the right decisions, at the right time... who knows? Now I just think *c'est la vie*, that's just the way it is.

With any script I get, I sit down and evaluate it. I try and decide what, if anything, is good about it, all the time considering which might be the best part for me – not always the one I'm being offered.

Say *you* were an actor, how would you look at *this* book if it were a script? Your agent got it first, and now they've sent it to you. The agent tells you what role they think you should play, but then you read it and think well, there's a nice cameo here and there but the main character is a bit of a pain in the arse. He gets a few laughs but usually at other people's expense!

Every time, before you even read that first page, you just can't help thinking, this could be *the* script. This one could change my life. Of course, alternatively, it could be the utter turkey that steers your promising career into a dreaded dead end. If you do decide to do the play, film, sitcom or whatever, rarely will it be something that just slots seamlessly into place with no effect on the order of your existence. It can change your life, change your geography, your finances, your outlook, your philosophy, your friends or even your partner. It's radical stuff, it's a big deal, it's a bloody nightmare.

Inevitably (well, inevitable if you're me), once you've decided to take a role, at some point soon you'll have a crisis of confidence; you'll panic that you've just made the worst mistake of your career. You *always* change your mind. I don't think I've ever taken on a script, with the possible exception of *GBH*, and been resolutely fixed on my decision. There's always an element of uncertainty. Will it work? Can it work? You try and gauge what other people's opinion of it will be, but most importantly, you have to ask yourself, 'What do I honestly think of it?'

The title of Jake Ebert's book about Goldcrest Films encapsulates it brilliantly: *My Indecision is Final*. I'm sure I've even said that to my agent at some point, along with "it's a definite maybe" or the Sam Goldwynism "include me out". But Jane Howell was right: "Trust your instinct."

Me and My Girl was definitely, no maybe, a 'definite maybe' when I first got the script. At the same time that I was being asked to do it, I was also offered a Russian touring production of *The Lower Depths* with the director Lyubimov. I had a decision to make: whether to do the serious, worthy slice of classic Gorky or this quaint musical called *Me and My Girl*. For some reason I chose *Me and My Girl*. For the life of me, I can't remember exactly why, although I suspect the sheer, dogged persistence of David Aukin (ably assisted by the brilliant director Mike Ockrent) had a lot to do with it.

Me and My Girl was three years of my life, beginning in Leicester in 1984. I opened the show at the Adelphi in the West End in January 1985, and then left the London show in February 1986 and went out to the USA where, after rehearsal in New York and a try-out run in Los Angeles, I opened on Broadway on 10 August 1986.

Although I accepted the role rather reluctantly – thinking that perhaps I was making a terrible mistake – and although I had to travel up to Leicester to some distinctly low-key church rehearsal rooms, when I was actually there I started thinking that this wasn't too bad. There was music, laughter, chorus girls in lycra and an old friend, Emma Thompson, to play opposite me. Things began to look up.

I never felt at Leicester that the show was going to be a hit as it was such an old musical (the original was written in the 1930s). The omens weren't good when we took it to the West End either. On my birthday in 1984, just before we opened in London, I was given a copy of *The Times* for the date of my birth, 13 December 1949. I turned, inevitably, to the arts page and there was a scathing review of a production of *Me and My Girl*. It was the actor Lupino Lane trying to resurrect the show in Brighton, having been so triumphant in it years earlier. He'd evidently tried to mount a successful revival in 1949 but it failed. I thought, this is it, what a bad omen – I'm going to die a death in this show!

In the event the reverse happened – it was a monster hit. That opening night in London we got a standing ovation. We all did the curtain call and we were bowing together when Frank Thornton, who played Sir John Tremayne in the show, made me come forward. People were stamping their feet and Frank knew, being so experienced, that the show was a major hit. He pushed *me* forward as he gestured to everyone else in the cast to step back. The whole audience was on its feet and I just thought, 'Oh, my God! Oh, my God! This is big!' Until that moment, I didn't fully realise what kind of show we had on our hands. I hadn't been able to gauge it, simply because audiences outside London can be very different from those in the West End.

I've often wondered what it was about the show that made it such a success. I think it was all down to its innocence, to its sense of good old-fashioned fun. It was the mid 1980s: there had been a drop in people's spirit with talk of a recession and, with Thatcher going in hard against the unions, the miners' strike had rekindled thoughts of Ted Heath's three-day week a decade earlier. When we opened in London, Emma was even pictured with a group of miners in her flat in West Hampstead. When I told my dad that I had to choose between *Me and My Girl* and *The Lower Depths* he'd said, "If you've got any sense, you'll do the musical. It'll cheer people up. It's just what they need in this country at the moment." When Dad came down to see it, he said, "I told you. Didn't it make you feel good?" They were so thrilled. I think that was when Mum and Dad suddenly realised the power of what was happening to my career.

Of course, we had to work really hard at the show to make it a success, and most of that hard work came during the rehearsal period, a period that was just glorious – I loved it!

Whatever I'm doing, the rehearsal phase is essential to the way I like to work. Beforehand, on my own, I can address the physical attributes of the characters and start to think about how I'm going to play them, but I can't learn the lines. I can only do that on set in rehearsal with the other actors; it's only when the character develops that the lines start to come. So I can't sit and study them, learning them by rote – I've never been able to do that. As soon as I start to interact with the other actors the lines do tend to come terribly easily. The difficulty arises when I'm down to a short rehearsal period, really motoring through it, then I have to work really hard to master the lines although my early stint in weekly rep did help.

If you try and learn the part just sitting at home, there's a danger that you won't really understand the sense of it, you won't grasp how it fits in with the overall play. Instead, the script simply becomes a series of lines, which means that if you lose your place during a performance you've got no way back. You have to find your way back through rehearsal. You have to *know* what the character would do, should you happen to forget a line. When you reach that point, anything can happen on stage and you won't lose it.

The rehearsal period is crucial for another reason – it's when you get to work with the director. That's particularly important for me because of the insecurities I have about my education; anxieties that go all the way back to Gladstone Boys' and failing the eleven-plus. Inevitably I come up against things that I don't understand. It happened a lot more when I was younger. That's when you need a director to unravel it for you and to say, "Well, try this."

During the rehearsal period the director will push you this way and that, moulding your character to fit the shape of the play. Michael Elliott once asked me, "How much do you hate?" "What?" I said. "How much do you hate?" he repeated. "Do you have *any* hate inside you? Do you hate anyone?" "No," I smiled. "Well, you need to find some hate in yourself to play this character, otherwise you'll never, ever get the audience to believe." He would come up really close to me each day and say, "I still can't see the hate Robert. Just let yourself go."

I tried training myself to think dark thoughts, until one morning in rehearsal I came in with my lines and Michael said, "I don't know who it is Robert, I don't know who you're hating, but it's not very pleasant. That's great!"

Getting that character right isn't just important to your own work, it's vital to the other members of the cast. Some actors talk rubbish about how all this conviction – or the lack of it – in another actor doesn't make any difference to their own part. If another actor in character is looking at you, you've got to be able to convince them that what you are doing is something that they can sympathise with or be frightened of. Similarly, if mem-

154

bers of the audience can see the joins, then they're going to get bored. With real actors, genuinely good actors, you can't see the cracks – the character feels real.

If the show works, these factors – the dialogue, the character, the ensemble – all come together. That's what happened with *Me and My Girl*; all the groundwork we put in during that rehearsal period in Leicester paid off.

The show's producers had put in extra numbers like 'Leaning on a Lamp Post' and a tap dance routine for 'Song of Hareford' but other than that, the show was more or less the same as it had been in the 1930s. And so Emma Thompson and I put in lots of 'business', those little touches that help bring it to life. We used to work for hours and hours into the night in the Leicester Holiday Inn. It was on a roundabout, but had a swimming pool, so you could watch the traffic going round while you were in the water!

Emma and I lived in each other's pockets and constantly worked on inventing stuff for the show. Emma was very good at all that – I think we both were – but we didn't get a lot of credit for how much we added to the production. We came up with all kinds of 'business': the falling over the chair, the catching of the cigarettes, and the bowler hat routine.

In one scene I came on wearing a cloak, so Emma suggested we use it as a prop, recalling how the witch in the *Wizard of Oz* had melted away into her own black cape. I developed this routine of swirling, hiding and moving, doing all these tricks with the cloak – it stopped the show! Meanwhile, the 'writers' were getting all this down, making it a part of the production.

Oh, the invention, the freedom. I watched loads of Keaton and Chaplin movies – noting the 'business' they used, studying the way they played to the audience, the little tricks and turns when something happened. I modelled some of what went into the show on those guys, and I realised later that Lupino Lane must have done so too. We'd both modelled bits of Bill Snibson on Charlie Chaplin.

I went into *Me and My Girl* with a real sense of innocence and fun. Having initially resisted involvement, when I did take the plunge I really gave in to it. I committed one hundred per cent – as I do with everything. One day at rehearsal, I put a white face on – like Chaplin used to do – which made Richard Armitage and David Aukin freak out. "Why are you doing that?" they asked. "Well it's the clown," I replied. They were insistent, saying, "But no, it's got to be you." And I countered: "But it's not me. I've never played this kind of character before. I don't do *me*. I play a character."

I did tone it down a bit in the end, but put the charcoal around my eyes like Chaplin did. I tried to use the look on *The Val Doon-ican Show* when Emma and I were invited to appear and perform a number. The make-up girls said, "It's going to look very odd on Saturday night television, especially with Emma looking really glamorous and you… looking like that." "But that's how I'm going to play it on stage," I told them. "Fine," they said, "but this is television on Saturday night at seven o'clock." I lost the battle – they made me up *their* way and I felt really uncomfortable. I always feel more at ease if I've made the character I play feel alien to me in some way, it makes it easier to 'become' the part.

On that TV appearance we showcased a song and dance routine. It went pretty much to plan, but one of the reasons I'd hesitated about doing *Me and My Girl* in the first place was because it was going to involve so much dancing. I hadn't really done any before. I had a few run-ins with the choreographer on the show, Gillian Gregory, because she was determined, as she had to be, to make me dance her way. She used to say, "You'll never, ever, be a dancer." I ended up winning the Astaire Award on Broadway, which, I have to say, became a bit of a family joke.

Gillian came to see me in *The Entertainer* many years later and said that she was still in shock that I'd won that dancing award in New York. She also said she'd bet me any money that I'd changed and changed the choreography in *The Entertainer* until I'd made it mine. She was right of course. It goes back to that thing of always wanting to make a role my own. In *Me and My Girl* she tried to make me do set dance sequences, which I could do, but I always had to make them 'me'. I remember her moaning about the soft shoe routine in 'Leaning on a Lamp Post'. "Not one of those was my steps in the end. You improvised it. And you know what? You could!" she said. "I used to watch you and think, I'm going to give him some notes, but how could I give you notes – you'd changed all my steps!"

I hadn't done any dancing before, but I knew that I was fairly physically adept. By that, I mean I could move! I'd been in a musical down in Exeter and was reasonably good at movement and mime – so I knew I was capable of doing the stuff. I'd also done a bit of sword fencing, which involves a lot of footwork. But I'm not a dancer. I can't do a routine. I can't really learn, memorise and repeat it accurately. My wife Rosemarie *is* a dancer and can still remember routines that she did in the 1970s. It's as if she's got 'muscle memory'. She once went in and did the musical *Cats* at very short notice, having not done it for five years. They rang her up and asked her to play the lead because a flu epidemic (cat flu

– sorry, couldn't resist it!) had struck the cast on tour. She went off and just danced it, just like that, straight away. Now that's the difference between dancers and actors. Dancers are almost mathematical in that sense, learning it all by rote.

Unsurprisingly, when I went up to Leicester to start rehearsals for *Me and My Girl,* I was more than a little bit nervous about having to do the dancing, especially the tap routines. Tap steps I couldn't change, of course, and we had to have a crash course in how to do them. On opening night in Leicester I remember a general sense of amazement that I'd actually pulled the dance steps off, that I hadn't fallen flat on my face at any stage, particularly during the tap routines. "I just couldn't believe you'd done it," Diana said. "When you came back and rehearsed in the kitchen at home, I used to think, 'Oh God! Perhaps he shouldn't be doing this.' But not only did you do it, you made it your own and looked like you'd been doing it all your life."

At the Adelphi, the company for *Me and My Girl* settled in to the run of the show and it became a hugely enjoyable experience. The theatre itself – as you may know if you've ever been there – was almost like an extra character. It's a bit spooky, to say the least. I got into the habit of throwing after-show parties in my dressing room, which they'd recently revamped. That was alright, but there was another dressing room at the theatre that was seriously haunted. It was right down in the bowels of the theatre – I don't think they use it anymore other than as a storeroom. My dog Yak (for 'Iach', named after Iachimo in *Cymbeline*) was always really strange about that room, simply refusing to go in it. Emma Thompson and I did a charity performance for the Royal Variety Show in the theatre one night and we had to stay there late. We both experienced some very weird sensations, to the extent that we got out of the building as soon as we could.

Richard Armitage, the producer of *Me and My Girl*, even went as far as getting the Adelphi blessed because of the fears about the place being haunted and the lack of recent success. We all stood round in a circle with the priest carrying out the blessing.

One story adds to the Adelphi's dark legend more than most. In 1897 William Terriss, a famous nineteenth-century actor, was stabbed to death at the stage door of the theatre. As you would expect, his ghost is now said to walk the rooms backstage. Whatever the truth, the tale of William Terriss found an eerie parallel in one of my own backstage experiences at the theatre. In short, some guy tried to kill me.

The bloke in question was involved in the show and married to one of the chorus girls. One Saturday evening, right in the middle of one of my dressing-room parties, I suddenly found this guy's arms around my neck. He was trying to strangle me, having turned up all 'tired and emotional' and mistakenly presumed that I was having an affair with his wife.

That, supposedly, is what happened to William Terriss. He was thought to be having an affair with the wife of his understudy who then stabbed him through the heart. Thankfully, my own experience stopped short of such a dramatic conclusion. The guy was a real bear of a man and was squeezing the life out of me. Eventually, other guests managed to pull him off me and out of the room and away he went down the stairs, shouting, with his wife screaming after him. I just sat there on the sofa shaking, with everyone offering me a drink, a brandy, just calming me down. It was ghastly... and ever so slightly ghostly! I suppose I should be glad I didn't the go the way of old William Terriss...

THIRTEEN

NIGHTS ON BROADWAY

I DIDN'T miss a single scheduled performance of *Me and My Girl* in London, and that was doing all eight shows a week for over fifty-two weeks. It did so well they decided they were going to take the show to Broadway – quite a bold move for such an English style of musical. The thinking must have been that 'quintessentially English' would work in New York.

The Americans used to call it *Me and My Gal* and, as a result, they all thought that it featured the song 'For Me and My Gal', as in 'the bells are ringing for me and my girl'. All *I* could think was that I was going to be doing 'The Lambeth Walk' on Broadway!

The absurdity of taking cockney London to the New Yorkers was subsequently lampooned brilliantly in *Forbidden Broadway*, a long-running satirical off-Broadway revue. They invited us to see what they were doing, so I went along with some mates from the show. They gave us front row seats, served us dinner and really looked after us. They did a whole sequence sending up the show and 'me and my reviews'. The *New York Times* theatre critic, Frank Rich, had written: "Mr Lindsay... (has been) miraculously discovered among the mere mortals of today". So the *Forbidden Broadway* guys did this whole thing about me being an alien. They went into 'The Lambeth Walk', the gag being: 'Any time you're Lambeth way, any evening any day, you'll find us all, doing the Lambeth walk... here we go again... Any time you're Lambeth way... Any time you're...' and on and on and on, until they were all lying on the floor asleep and the music was still playing. It was a very funny send-up indeed. They don't know how near the truth they were.

I really enjoyed working with Stanley Lebowsky, the musical director for the Broadway production of *Me and My Girl*. In what must have been one of the first rehearsals, I can remember him saying to me in his thick Bronx accent, "C'mon Robert, let's get Broadway. Let's think big."

He sang to me as a Mafioso godfather soundalike: "Hold my ha-a-a-nd." Then he said, "OK, e-x-t-e-n-d Robert, extend it."

I did just as he'd done, or so I thought: "Hold my ha-a-a-nd..." and got: "NO! Let go... let's go Broadway!"

Stanley was renowned for being horrific to cast members when he was teaching them songs, but he was a brilliant musical director, not least because he'd done every major show on Broadway. He looked like a bulldog and behaved like a terrier – the female cast members were frequently in tears or running off stage – but he knew he'd met his match with me. I did used to tease him: "Hold my ha-a-a-nd..." indeed! But I had the upper hand because this was an English musical and a bit foreign to him.

There was another line he had problems with where I had to say that someone was "Hovis".

"Robert, what's Hovis?"

So I tried to explain the cockney rhyming slang of Hovis, brown bread, dead! So, "My parents are Hovis."

Stanley stared at me in total bemusement before he finally said: "Robert, this is America. Instead of Hovis, can you say wholewheat or maybe rye?"

For all that, he was absolutely the man for the job. If you take a quaint English musical from the 1930s and you put it on Broadway in the 1980s then you have to get *the* top Broadway musical director, the guy who's done everything from *Chicago* through to *West Side Story*.

"OK Robert, from the top, we're going to do 'Me and My Girl', OK? Not Me and My Gal, Me and My Goiirrll. OK, Robert, let's go!"

So off I went: "Me and my girl made for each other..."

"No, Robert, goirl. Me and my goiirrll!"

And again: "Me and my goiirrll, meant for each other, sent for each o-ther and likin' it so..."

Finally, some good feedback: "That's good Robert, that's good!"

"Stanley, isn't it a little aggressive?"

"You're on Broadway now, Robert."

It was great stuff. God love him. I loved him. Good old Stanley Lebowsky.

He used to say to say to me: "Mr Oh-liv-e-ay-A-ward-Lind-say. You won an Oh-liv-e-ay A-ward. Really? That makes you a big shot?"

He'd really try and put you down: "Well this is Broadway now, Bob! We're gonna make it Broadway."

"So how do we make 'The Lambeth Walk' 'Broadway', Stanley?" I'd ask cheekily.

And he'd huff back: "We've gotta lotta work to do, Bob!"

When he did 'The Sun Has Got His Hat On' with the rest of the cast, I used to stand at the back, watching these chorus kids – more used to doing shows like *A Chorus Line* and *Chicago* – doing the tap routine and singing brightly this very English song: "The sun has got his hat on, hip, hip, hip hooray."

Next you'd hear this gruff New York accent shouting: "NO, NO it's hip, hip, hip *hoo-RAY!!!*" There were girls crying and walking out. I'd be pissing myself laughing at the back and all I could see were these glasses, Stanley's glasses, staring back at me. "This is Broadway, Bob."

We spent five or six weeks rehearsing at the studios of Michael Bennett. Michael had directed *A Chorus Line*, and that show's composer, Marvin Hamlisch, had been to see *Me and My Girl* in London. I had a lot of time for Marvin, a very clever guy, although he had a few strange ideas – he wanted me to get Stanley to put drawing pins in the piano so that it would make that authentic 'honky-tonk' sound. I've got letters from him saying *please* get them to recreate that old English sound.

Of course, Stanley Lebowsky and Chris Walker, who'd done the musical direction for the show in England and was now working with us in New York, were desperately trying to turn *Me and My Girl* into a really big romantic musical for the American audiences. They re-orchestrated it, and the orchestra in the States was extraordinary. When we heard the first sitzprobe (that's what they call the first seated rehearsal with full orchestra) on Broadway, well, Richard Armitage wept, hearing the music his father, Noel Gay (the creative impresario and the man behind the original show), had composed played in such wonderful arrangements.

The whole company upped and went off to LA after the studio

rehearsal period in New York. It was fabulous. It was like *Some Like It Hot* with the whole company travelling together. We were a very close-knit group of people; in fact we still are, and keep in touch with each other through reunions from time to time.

As we set off for California one of the cast said to me, "Let's hope it's not a hit in LA." When I asked why, he replied, "Because then, we'll be *BIG* in New York!"

I was staying in The Biltmore in downtown LA when the local reviews came out. Incidentally, it was an awful place to be staying. Not the hotel, which was nice, but downtown LA. It should have been Beverly Hills, and that's where I moved to eventually. Anyway, the LA reviews were rather lukewarm. They were very positive about my performance, but unenthusiastic about the show as a whole. It was doing OK but it wasn't playing to packed houses. I think this was partly because the theatre we were in was just too big. It was the Dorothy Chandler Pavilion, where they used to hold the Oscars ceremony. It was a three thousand-seater, which we only half-filled at most. The actor George S Irving and I used to fly aeroplanes in it. He was an ex-fighter pilot from the Second World War and, a bit like John Wayne, he was a big guy. We used to have this passion: the two of us would throw paper aeroplanes all the way across the theatre onto the stage. That's what we spent our days doing. Being completely loopy, almost loop the loopy.

In that huge barn of a place, people had to use binoculars and telescopes to look down at the stage – opera glasses simply weren't man enough for the job. I thought, 'This is awful. That's it. I shouldn't have done it. I shouldn't have come to America!' But the good old cast member just kept saying, "We're going to be *BIG* in New York."

We had a strange time in LA. After doing the show to a half-empty theatre, we'd go out to a deserted town where every bar was empty and every restaurant was closing up – it was a world apart from London or New York in that respect. Going out after the show trying to swank didn't work. LA is closed at ten o'clock – or Beverly Hills is at least. It being 'Movie Central', everyone is in bed. If you're seen out after ten o'clock at night, it means you're not working, so I couldn't even show off, I just had to get on with it.

We did LA for about seven or eight weeks and then I came home to England for a bit of the summer, probably about a week and a half, until I had to go back to rehearse for the New York opening. Before the cast had left to do the run in LA, we'd performed a snippet of the show on stage in New York for a select audience and the response hadn't been great. So, when we returned, I really thought we were going to die a death, especially after the LA experience. I'd heard horror stories about shows closing on the first night and thought, 'Well, that could be me.'

When I got back over to New York I didn't even bother to unpack my suitcase at the Wyndham Hotel. Didn't hang up a suit; didn't put a shirt in the wardrobe. Everything stayed in my suitcase with my passport on the top. I thought I was going home so what was the point of unpacking?

And then everything went crazy. We opened on 10 August 1986 to unprecedented reviews and that same cast member came bouncing up to me and said: "Didn't I tell you we were going to be *BIG* in New York?"

On the first night they put up a neon newsflash outside the theatre in Times Square that read "...and we welcome to Broadway the greatest... our new star, Robert Lindsay", quoting the Frank

Rich review. Diana and I read it standing in the pouring rain as a huge thunderstorm broke overhead. We went to an incredible after-show party: three thousand people in an enormous ballroom. All my family and friends came along, having made the trip over for opening night.

After the party, as we celebrated and read the reviews, it began to hit me that the show would be going on and I would be staying in New York. It was everyone else who would be going home the next day. My partner was going home. My parents and my brother were going home. My best friends were all leaving.

In Central Park the following day, my head was clouded with doubt and homesickness. We all went for brunch before everyone headed off to JFK to catch evening flights to Gatwick and Heathrow. Walking back through the park with Diana after brunch I broke down in tears. She asked what the matter was. "You're all going home. I'm here on my own. F***! It's a hit!" "Yes, isn't it wonderful?" she said, but there I was, wailing about wanting to go home. See what I mean? I find it difficult to enjoy success.

But, I'd done it. I'd done it! All I had to do now was to keep on doing it. I was in *Me and My Girl* for over a year in the USA, and Diana came over to live with me in New York for most of my time there. I think it was difficult for her. She tried to keep up with my adrenaline levels so much that she kind of overtook me and immersed herself in the social scene, in the endless round of parties. Everyone was using cocaine. It was incredibly widespread. Throwing a party after we'd done a charity show in the theatre one Sunday evening after the matinee, I walked into my dressing room and it looked like every member of the cast was in there, all tooting coke. This really was 'Freedom for Tooting'. All over again!

Endless parties, interviews, backstage visits… every night, every day. I had to employ a PA, Suzanne Golden, just to keep things organised. She wasn't very popular with the rest of the company because she separated me from them when, previously, I had been such a company man. Until then, they had all had a piece of me, but suddenly Suzanne started pulling me away, managing the demands on me and my time that seemed to grow and grow. Richard Armitage and the management obviously told her to get me out of the theatre and get me home after each show – to make sure I had a car booked and to make sure that I got in it.

My life was suddenly quite organised. Suzanne didn't drink and didn't party; she just watched, was always there, and drove everyone in the company crazy. She was a terrific PA, knew a lot of people and was wonderful at 'screening' the dressing room and the stage door, only letting the 'right' people in. It was a vital skill because in the States, unlike in the UK, people visit you backstage during the interval, when it's all happening, when everything's totally frenetic – can you believe it?

On any one day I could have Burt Lancaster, Kirk Douglas, Margot Fonteyn, Sean Connery, Lauren Bacall, Gregory Peck or Barbra Streisand in my dressing room at the interval. The show's management would have their press people there bringing photographers in, so I'd do a photo with whichever star had turned up. I'd be sweating from doing the show and the visitors would be asking, "Are you going to have a drink?" "No, sorry, I can't," I would say. "I've got another hour to do."

The big stars couldn't come in at the end of the show because members of the audience would be milling around by then and there'd be a gaggle of people waiting backstage and at the stage door. So, the famous folk would invariably come backstage at the interval, have a photo and provide a quote about how brilliant the show was for the next day's *New York Times*, where the Diary page would record who'd visited Robert Lindsay's dressing room the night before.

My time in New York was very special. It wasn't just because the show did well; it had more to do with the things that happened to me, and the people that came in and out of my life. Of all those people, Katharine Hepburn probably made the greatest impression.

She came to see the show four times. One of the guys in the cast spotted her in the audience and told me about it. "I thought I'd tell you that Katharine Hepburn has been to see the show three times," he said. "She always wears a headscarf and dark glasses and sits in the same seat."

Alan Shallcross, a TV producer friend of mine who knew Katharine, came backstage one night and said, "Katharine is dying to meet you. She's wondering if she could take you out for supper or maybe you could go to her home." The arranged night duly came and she sat in her usual seat wearing the headscarf and dark glasses. The chorus boy said to me, "She's in again!" I tried to look casual: "I know. I'm going out for dinner with her." He gasped, "You're going out for dinner with Katharine Hepburn? Oh my God!"

Diana was invited as well. She went on ahead of me to Katharine's apartment, while Katharine herself came to meet me after the show with her driver-cum-housekeeper-cum-personal assistant, a lovely, charming guy named Henry, who obviously adored her. I started signing autographs at the stage door, but she came up and grabbed me and pulled me into the car. "Don't keep me waiting any longer," she snapped. "And why are you signing autographs? You've thanked them. They've thanked you. You've had a curtain call. That's what curtain calls are for. Now get on with your real life."

Anyway, she took me home. Diana was already there with Katharine's nieces. We had a little light supper. She kept pouring me doubles of malt whisky, one after the other. She was drinking it too, telling me how Spencer Tracy had loved malt whisky.

Later that night we danced in the communal garden of her brownstone on the Upper East Side. It was a beautiful garden with mature trees that were all lit up. We danced to the music playing in her place, getting further and further away from the house as we were dancing. "I've wanted to do this with someone for so many years," she said. "When I saw you on that stage, I knew I wanted to dance with you."

Meanwhile, in another room, Diana sat with the three nieces or 'the three witches' as she called them, who were keeping her away from Katharine and me. An eighty-year-old woman was innocently flirting with me in her garden whilst my partner was stuck in her apartment. As we started getting well away from the house, the music in the apartment began losing out to the sounds of someone playing a piano nearby. It was like someone was warming up, playing scales and searching for notes. Katharine called out, "Stephen! Shut up!" "Who's that?" I asked. "You know, Stephen?" "Stephen?" I enquired. "Sondheim. He drives me crazy when he does that."

She told me a story about when she was burgled. She never locked her door, which seemed pure folly to me in New York. When we first arrived at the apartment we'd been able to walk straight in through the front door without unlocking it. I asked if she ever worried about people breaking in. "They don't have to break in, it's open." I thought that was a bit eccentric, but of course didn't say as much. "We were burgled once," she continued. "I discovered them on the landing holding all my stuff. There was one black guy and one white guy and I approached them carrying my candle. I calmly said to them, 'What are you doing?' The white guy gaped and said, 'Oh my God, it's you!' They put the stuff down and left. They all think I'm a saint or something."

Diana said she didn't know why she didn't go straight home because she could tell at once that Katharine didn't want her there at all. She said the whole reason for the nieces being there was to keep her occupied. In truth it was a good job Diana *was* there to help me home – I was blotto by the time we left. So blotto in fact, that it all seems like a dream to me now.

The night Michael Jackson came to see me backstage was, in contrast, simply surreal. When word got round that he was coming backstage after a performance, all the kids in the chorus wanted to say hello but Suzanne vetoed it. No wonder she wasn't everyone's Little Miss Favourite. Michael was in my dressing room having tea with me for forty minutes. He was with Quincy Jones – they'd been to see the show together.

Michael was fascinated by the show and its old-fashioned innocence. He took great interest in my appearance: the white face and charcoal-lined eyes, the above-the-ankle-length trousers, white socks and patent leather shoes. He was particularly intrigued that I had studied mime at RADA. I told him I had been very influenced by Keaton and Chaplin, Jacques Tati, Marcel Marceau and Gene Kelly. He became very animated at the mention of such names and I realised then that he was a lot more than just a pop star – he was a very serious performer indeed.

At one point Michael asked me if he could use the phone. "Yeah sure," I said. "Just dial nine for an outside line." Michael was saying into the phone, "Yeah, OK, can I just say goodnight. Yeah. Goodnight baby. Robert, do you want to say goodnight to Bubbles?" I whispered to Quincy, "Who's Bubbles?" and Quincy said, humouring Michael, "It's Michael's chimpanzee. Just say goodnight. It won't hurt. It's OK." So I went over, took the phone and said: "Hi, it's Robert's here." And I could hear these noises at the other end… coming from the chimp! Michael Jackson had asked me to say goodnight to a chimpanzee and there I was doing exactly as he requested. Who was mad? Him or me?

Not long after that night I was in Washington doing a performance at the Kennedy Center Honors (an annual performing arts awards ceremony which that year was honouring, amongst others, Lucille Ball, Jessica Tandy, Stevie Wonder and Ray Charles), and met up with Quincy Jones again. In the way things are, he and I were by now, in showbiz terms, 'good friends' (in other words, we had met once before!). "You're amazing, man," he said. "What?" "You are amazing," he repeated. "Thanks," I said, smiling inanely, until he cut in with, "No, I don't mean that, I mean the shit you gave Michael. You really did it, didn't you. You really spoke to Bubbles. I didn't believe you'd do it." "Wasn't I supposed to?" I asked. "He's totally out there man." Quincy said this in an affectionate rather than a derogatory way as he obviously adored Michael. "He's so whacky and you fell for it!" 'Oh my God,' I thought, 'Quincy Jones thinks I'm a proverbial English twit.' He then reassured me: "No, it was fine, you were great, don't worry… but you did say goodnight to a chimp!"

By this point, it was all starting to get a bit out of hand in

New York. Michael Jackson, Katharine Hepburn – I even went to an amazing party hosted by Ronald and Nancy Reagan – perhaps I was starting to believe all the hype, perhaps it was all beginning to go to my head. Looking back, I can see that I needed to have my arse kicked – I needed that peculiarly English way of dealing with success.

I suppose the real tragedy was that I didn't wait around for the *Me and My Girl* movie to be made. Alas, the moment had kind of passed by the time I discovered that Steven Spielberg was very interested in getting the rights, as indeed was Paul Newman, who I'd met in New York one evening when he came to see the show. He later sent me footage of 'The Lambeth Walk' that Lupino Lane did, which he'd discovered in an archive. His accompanying note said, 'You know you've really got to do the movie of this because it is going to be a big hit'.

But I was too confused. My success in New York had brought a flood of other offers, and I couldn't and wouldn't wait. I stupidly grabbed the first thing that came along, which was *Bert Rigby, You're a Fool*, a film written and directed by Carl Reiner, a big Hollywood name back then.

I'm sure my story is similar to that of many an actor who has made it big on Broadway. It's very hard, impossible really, to explain what happens to you there when you have that kind of success. I don't know how I managed to keep my head straight at all really, meeting the great and the good of show business and being offered all these amazing things. It's startling to think that it all started in the Leicester rehearsal rooms and went on to reach that kind of euphoria in New York.

FOURTEEN

GETTING EMOTIONAL

SADLY, EVEN after all these years, my memories of *Me and My Girl* are coloured somewhat by irritation. In this business things have a tendency of going a bit sour when the show you're in starts making big money. And *Me and My Girl* in New York did make some serious money – it was a monster success.

The show ran for seven and a half years in London in a two thousand-seater theatre. In New York, it ran for over a year in a three thousand-seater at fifty bucks a ticket! I don't remember ever playing that show to an empty seat. I suppose my irritation stems from the feeling that I wasn't recognised for my role in this success.

Before and during the show I built up a good relationship with the producer Richard Armitage (known as RA to his friends). I felt the whole thing was very much a personal journey for both him and me. However, the main credit – as is usual – went to Mike Ockrent, the director, and to Stephen Fry, who was taken on to adapt and update the original 'book' of the musical, as written by Arthur Rose and Douglas Furber. Mike and Stephen tweaked it and put in extra numbers like 'Leaning on a Lamp Post' (another Noel Gay song), something they were able to do because RA had the rights to all the music.

Arthur Rose actually befriended me during the production (he was pretty elderly by that point). He felt he'd been airbrushed out of the new show and under-acknowledged for his contribution. After all, he did co-write the original book.

I think the 'business' that actors put into a performance can make a huge creative contribution to the production. I've already mentioned the research that I did for the part, and all the 'business' that Emma and I invented during the rehearsal period in Leicester. The famous cloak scene, for example, had no real instruction written down for it at all. It said something to the effect of 'He comes on in a long cloak and a crown', but I knew from my dad that in the original show, Lupino Lane made this into a ten-minute scene. Unfortunately Dad couldn't remember what Lane actually did to fill those ten minutes. But Mike Ockrent and Stephen Fry didn't know either, so we invented it all: the rolling off the sofa, catching the cigarette in my mouth, catching the bowler hat when I went over... all the schtick. In fact, we invented so much 'business', that when Mike Ockrent came to see me in New York he left a note in my dressing room that said: "If you invent any more 'business', Robert, you will disappear up your own arse."

It reached the stage where I began to question why I wasn't getting a 'point' (a share of the box office) for the show. I knew Mike and Stephen were, justifiably, doing very well financially out of it and, although I was earning a good fee, I wasn't sharing directly in the box office success and the profits that were pouring in. I kept thinking, 'Hang on, I've done all this work, all this groundwork, and I'm not really getting the financial recognition for it.' I know this is pretty standard stuff – it happens all the time in this industry – but that still didn't prevent the feeling of irritation building up, particularly at a time when I was coming to the end of my run and knew the part would be going to someone else – leaving me without work.

It came to a head when RA visited me in New York in the autumn of 1986. He said, "Robert, you're like a son to me and I am really proud of our association. I'd like to recognise your contribution to the show's success." I thought I was set to make a great deal of money from the show that was being sold all over the world by then but, a week later, RA died.

I was truly devastated. For the time being, my ongoing financial involvement was forgotten. I felt so alone as his death had come as a terrible blow. We'd gone on such a journey together and he'd been wonderful as a friend and mentor. I wept so much the day I was told he'd died. I was inconsolable. The sense of loss was overwhelming.

But as the weeks went by, the dull realisation came that nothing had been sorted out legally about my future earnings from the show. All I had was a proposal from poor old RA, and obviously that didn't get me very far. The whole experience left me somewhat disillusioned, but I knew that it would eat me away and I needed to let it go.

The trouble is, I can't *not* put that creativity into a part or a piece that I'm doing. Whether it's TV like *My Family* or *Citizen Smith,* or in the theatre in *Me and My Girl* or *The Entertainer*, there's always this 'stuff' that I put in. I feel like I'm semi-directing, being a hands-on performer. I suppose I always feel like I have to be in control of a piece, and when I get to have that all-important role in the end product, it is very satisfying. Fortunately, that satisfaction is usually its own reward. However, after all that graft it would be nice to have something lasting to show for it. At the end of a production I sometimes feel that (to use an old saying) 'once the gold mine as been closed down and the gold has gone, all that I'm left with is the shaft!'

All that 'business' stuff, the invention that I try and bring to a role, is intrinsic to the way I approach acting – it's all about building a character. There have been numerous occasions in my career when people have said, "We just want you to be you." It's happens a lot when I do voice-overs. "No we don't want you to do that. Can you just be you?" they say. And I respond: "I don't know who *I* am, I'm sorry, but I do know who I want to be in this."

I know actors say that kind of thing a lot – that they don't really know who they are – but it's certainly been a dominant feature all the way through my career, that confusion over identity. Of course, in a simplistic sense I know who I am: I am Robert Stevenson; I come from a council estate in the Midlands; the son of a joiner and a cleaner. However, ask me to look deeper, beyond that shaping influence of environment, and I struggle.

I've always been acting in one respect or another. Earlier in life, before I did it for a job, I would be living in my imagination, playing some imaginary part or other. I can see the same thing now in Sam, my son. "He isn't *going* to be an actor, he *is* an actor," my wife Rosie recently said of Sam. What did she mean? Simply that Sam acts things out in his imagination and sometimes lives in a fantasy world (just like I did as a child). He's a very sensitive soul and very perceptive about emotions. He's also a brilliant mimic. I've seen him be something completely other than himself. He can make a facial expression and a gesture and I say, "Sam are you alright?" "Yeah," he replies. "I'm just acting." It's terrifying.

That combination of imagination and perception is really what acting is all about: it's about being receptive to emotions, it's about absorbing them and then processing the information and presenting it in a character. I've seen the same abilities in my daughter Syd, so it looks like they have both inherited that gene.

In truth, a lot of acting is about deceiving people. You could call it lying. Well, maybe lying is a bit strong, but it's not far off; you're hiding your real thoughts and your real emotions and becoming something else altogether. Olivier knew it. He wasn't really a 'feeling' actor, but he was a very brilliant technician. John Osborne, who wrote *The Entertainer*, knew it too.

Archie Rice sums it up in a great speech in *The Entertainer* when he says he doesn't feel a thing: "If you learn it properly you'll get yourself a technique. You can smile, darn you, smile, and look the friendliest jolliest thing in the world..."

Olivier was a master at that. When I worked with him I noticed how clever he was at changing his voice and using it in such a way that you really thought he was emoting. He showed how using the pitch of the voice works as another means of conveying emotion, provided you have the skills to do it. He would use the timbre of speech to convey an emotion that he wasn't really feeling.

The more I think about my work, the more I feel that, in the main, I'm a naturalistic actor. Initially I just let go and try and inhabit the role, rather than trying to find the character through endless research and study, or by trying to look absolutely perfect in the part. Of course, I've also picked up a lot of technique along the way from comedy, light entertainment, musicals, film, television and straight theatre, but it usually takes second place to the naturalism.

Some actors are all about the emotion. Richard Harris was like that – he invested real passion in everything he did. I think that's why he found actors like Michael Caine hard to take. I remember Richard Harris launching into a huge tirade about Michael because, to him, he didn't seem to 'feel' anything.

Then there are actors like Peter O'Toole, Richard Burton and Nicol Williamson who are considered to be more of a blend, a mixture of emotion and technique. Usually though, actors are one or the other – 'technical' or 'emotional' – and there is a big difference between the two. Of course, it also happens that the 'technicians' evolve and become more emotional and the emotional ones start going all technical. I think I've gone from being a spontaneous, emotional actor to one who has picked up an awful lot of technique. If I'd stayed on the path of being purely emotional I would probably be dead by now. You can't survive like that. In the end, if you're doing a long run in a production, you've got to find the technique to get you through it. You have to find a way of 'pulling back'. Not cheating the audience, but not giving your absolute all either. You do this by using your voice in a different way, or using a physical gesture to make something look threatening, as opposed to drenching everything in emotion and physicality.

In one production I watched a young actress who had to cry in a particular scene produce genuine tears every time I did the big speech concerned. It was so generous of her. She was 'feeling' it and, as a result, was exhausted only four weeks into the run.

She told me that she'd never done anything as emotionally draining, and that she was sleeping through the day just to recover. Although I was looking a bit tired and snuffly after the same four weeks, I was basically fine, because I've found a way of not giving it everything.

Sometimes you can't help it. That release of emotion just overpowers you, as I learned to my cost once when I broke down during a play directed by Jane Howell. It was a production of the *Cornish Passion Play*, performed in a monastery in front of the abbots, abbesses, monks and nuns of Bodmin. At the end of the first act came the Crucifixion scene and, before the interval, we had to take Jesus down from the cross. The director decided that we all knew *how* He was crucified, but he wanted to depict what actually happened when they took Him down from the cross, thinking audiences would want to see it.

The idea was that we would take the nails out with claw hammers, Jesus would fall, we'd have someone catch Him and then the audience would watch, transfixed, as we removed the corpse. Then the music would start up and we'd go into the interval. So, there I was, playing John, the disciple, in front of two thousand devout people, all of them watching this amazing scene. It was my job to take out the second nail from one of His hands. The first nail had come out no problem, but mine wasn't as eager to surrender. I whispered, "I can't get it out. It's absolutely jammed in." Jesus was rather desperately saying, "Get it out! Get it out!"

We 'corpsed' and started sniggering. I was thinking, 'This is probably the most sacrilegious thing I've ever done, laughing at the removal of Christ from the cross (corpsing over the corpse if you will), in front of two thousand monastics.' Then, amid the chaos, a moment of clarity – I decided to turn the laughter into tears, to redirect the emotion if you like. It wasn't long before I was crying so badly that I couldn't do anything at all, and had to be carried away from the cross. I was the gibbering, sobbing wreck who left Jesus up there on the cross – "My God, why hast thou forsaken me?" Indeed.

While I'm on the subject of acting technique, I've often been asked what happens when I first get a script. What's going through my mind when I read it; am I visualising some fantasy end product? The answer is yes. I've usually got an overview of what I think it should look like, which is more of a director's eye view really. Then, through collaboration, the performance and the realisation of the character emerge. To me, collaboration equals overview plus working with the director and the other actors. However, sometimes the other actors don't fit the image that I've created in my head. When this happens I try and 'worm' them into acting in a way that does fit with my own ideas. Very naughty I know! I seem to be getting worse as I get older too. I've even been known to give other actors 'notes', with hints on how they might want to play a part.

I'm not sure how I get away with doing this (in fact, I'm not sure that I always do). In rehearsals for *The Entertainer* I suggested to John Normington, who was playing Archie Rice's father, that he should do a little dance routine as he comes downstage singing, "Rock of ages cleft for me, let me hide myself with thee". At first he just did it walking, but I said I thought it was too straight like that. You see he used to be an adulterer and a cheat (the character *not* John), but now, suddenly, he's found religion and so is full of beans. John changed it and afterwards came up to me, gave me a big hug and said, "Oh God! You were so right."

On other occasions I've met a brick wall, with actors saying, "Don't you tell me what to do... don't you dare presume to give me 'notes' on my performance." I know then that I'm not going to get on with them. It's not like I'm imposing on anyone. I'm just saying, "This is what I think. I don't know for certain, just try it." If I get an "um" in response I usually think 'this isn't going to run very long' or 'we're not going to gel'.

Obviously there are many times when I'm wrong, when I should bite my tongue. However, I've always felt that this business, particularly the theatre, is collaborative and, if I see something that could be improved, I have to speak out. Perhaps I should give directing a try!

FIFTEEN

ROBERT LINDSAY, YOU'RE A FOOL

WHEN *Me and My Girl* turned into a Broadway hit, Hollywood began knocking on the door. The offers came at me from every direction. Scripts came so thick and fast that my dressing room started to look like a giant in-tray. My dresser was even reading scripts for me. "Oh!" she'd say, "Warner Brothers have sent you this," or "Columbia have sent you that," or, "There's a huge TV piece on offer here."

A good move into films would have had an enormous effect on my career. Unfortunately, it didn't quite go to plan.

Things began going awry when I switched agents. When I first went over to New York, my agent, Felix de Wolfe, went with me. He tried desperately to introduce me to people – contacts, friends, producers and lawyers – but I felt that RA was in a much stronger position to help me because he knew the people that seemed to matter. In particular, he represented David Frost and so had done that transatlantic journey so many times. He seemed to be in the know; the people he was in touch with were influential, whereas Felix's contacts seemed to be old cronies who'd either retired or were about to. Has-beens, I suppose you could say.

Tragically, of course, RA then died and I was in limbo having left Felix. In the vacuum, the William Morris Agency moved in. They'd been courting me ever since my arrival in New York. Different members of the agency would turn up in my dressing room every night, and eventually I gave in to their encouragement and signed up. It was the fatal error of my time in America and, in fact, it turned out to be one of the biggest mistakes I ever made.

The thing about being a big hit in New York is that simply everyone comes at you. They all crawl out of the woodwork – accountants, lawyers, agents. And I didn't have anyone, I felt, who was protecting me. I was inviting everyone to my hotel room. I was having meetings with accountants: Zanuck this and Zanack that; and lawyers, Zimmabob this and Zimmerframe that. You name them, I met them. I'd give them tea and then the day after I'd get a bill from them for two thousand dollars! Monty Morris, a well-respected lawyer who RA had introduced me to, came in to protect me from all that. I soon became good friends with both Monty and his wife, Phyllis, who, incidentally, is godmother to my daughter.

It wasn't long before the William Morris Agency people – and in particular Katie Rothacker, a rather eccentric woman they had assigned to me – began pushing me in the wrong direction. I made the wrong decision, took the wrong film. I needed someone – someone like RA – saying to me "NO!" I think I would have gone in a different direction if RA had been alive. After being in a hit show in London and then on Broadway, perhaps with his guidance I would have had an international career. Who knows?

Instead, the 'Curse of the Successful Brit' hit me. The people at William Morris (and they had some pretty bizarre people) began talking about three quarters of a million dollars for a single project. No small fee today, but back in 1987 it was a phenomenal amount, particularly as it had only been a couple of years since I was doing *Hamlet* on £250 a week!

I suppose it's easy to blame an agent for pushing you into the wrong work – although I've never actually had one who's had the final say on anything, who's taken the ultimate decision on which project to pursue. Even so, I think all actors would like to feel that their agent would say "this is a bad idea" at the right time. However, I'm not sure all agents are actually capable of that. The cynical and sour-faced view is that it's what they can earn out of you in the short term that shapes their decisions, although it depends on the relationship you build with them.

The bottom line is always the main worry for an agent. If they get an amazing offer they will try and make it work, regardless of the negative effects on your long-term career. Maybe I'm guilty of generalising, because I think Felix de Wolfe genuinely cared for me and was desperately hurt when I left him. Felix might well have worked in cahoots with RA, had RA lived, because they liked each other and had a good relationship. But there was no way Felix was going to work with the William Morris Agency – he loathed them. My final exchange with the agency a few years later brought it home to me how different we were in outlook. They had a new guy in charge in London who took me out for dinner at The Ivy. "Right Robert," he said. "What is it that you want to do next?" I told him I didn't know. "First mistake," he said, and then rounded on me with, "We can't have people in the agency who don't know what they want to do." He was absolutely right – I left the next day.

In general, I've been quite loyal to agents. From RADA in 1970 I was with Marina Martin for five years, initially when she was with CCA and then subsequently when she set up Marina Martin Management. From Marina, I went to Felix and was with him for a good twelve years until I moved to William Morris. From them, I went to Hamilton Hodell. So, in total, it's only been four agents in a forty-year career.

Anyway, back in 1987, William Morris began flying me all over the place: to LA on my days off, or to Florida, or Connecticut. The things that were happening and the offers that were being made were absolutely unbelievable. I was being offered the world: this movie, that movie, this TV series, another major show. But, of course, the big thing, the big question, was whether I was going to do the 'bus and truck' of *Me and My Girl*, because that's where the big money lies, touring America. You can earn a lot of money on Broadway – I'd earned one million dollars in 1987 – but you can earn even more if you do the tour.

I didn't know what to do (as is the ditherer's prerogative). What I did know was that I was tired and wanted to finish the eight-shows-a-week treadmill of *Me and My Girl*. I know it's not working down a mine or anything, but there's still some serious graft involved. Some actors simply aren't prepared for it. Not long after I finished in *Me and My Girl* on Broadway I did a chat show with Brigitte Neilsen and Roger Moore. I was sitting in the VIP room with the two of them and Roger said to me: "I thought you were a big success in the States. Well done. Absolutely smashing." Coincidentally, at that time he was about to take on a role in a new West End musical. "Oh, thanks," I smiled. "The Andrew Lloyd Webber thing that you're going to do, that'll be great. Are you going to be alright doing eight shows a week?" He went, "I'm sorry?" then looked at his wife. She looked blank. "You *are* doing eight shows a week, aren't you?" I asked. He seemed rather shocked. Two days later it was in the newspapers that he'd dropped out of the show.

In my shower, every morning in New York, I was ticking off the shows that were left for me to do before I ended my contract, thinking, 'I've just got to get through it.' Diana was trying to enjoy our time in New York, but I just wanted to get the hell out. She was always busy entertaining our guests from England – and there seemed to be so many of them suddenly – when I was more interested in getting back to our apartment and going to bed. I just couldn't keep up. All I wanted was to get on with the job when I had to and then to lock myself away at other times. I didn't want to get drawn too deeply into the partying and the whole social thing, which was beginning to grind me down. When I look at photos of me taken after that year in New York, I look like something out of a prisoner-of-war camp – haggard, emaciated and wearing a rather haunted expression.

If I'd had more sense I would have gone home. But I had William Morris 'helping' me. And how did they help me? They introduced me to Carl Reiner!

When he appeared on the scene, I remember thinking he was a bit of a strange fellow, but the rest of the *Me and My Girl* cast said, "Carl Reiner! Don't you know who Carl Reiner is?" To which I could only reply, "No. I don't." "The director of Dick Van Dyck's TV shows, *The 2000 Year Old Man, Dead Men Don't Wear Plaid, The Man With Two Brains...*?" I looked suitably impressed: "Right then, so anything with 'Man' or 'Men' in the title and he's your guy?"

I got talking to Carl and a film project began to take shape. He started following me around New York, writing the script. I was asking myself if this was the right move, if I should be getting involved with the film. And all the time William Morris were telling me, "This could be good. This could be big."

What was weird was that he started writing down what he thought was my life story, but he kind of mistook my performance in *Me and My Girl* for the real me. I found that very strange about most Americans. Everyone who came backstage assumed that I was a real-life cockney chum – "Alright mate? Wanna cuppa tea? Cuppa char?" – despite me being myself and saying, "Actually, I'd prefer a glass of wine." Americans seem to think that you are what you act, no doubt because a lot of American actors probably do play themselves on screen or stage.

When Laurence Olivier was working on *Marathon Man* with Dustin Hoffman, and Hoffman was doing all that running and staying awake to get into the right 'state' for a scene, Olivier apparently looked at Hoffman and said, "Have you heard of acting dear boy?" It's a favourite line in the acting world, as indeed is Maggie Smith's, when she was asked in an interview what she thought of New York method acting. She said, "We have that same thing in England, it's called w***ing." I wish I'd said that!

Dustin Hoffman came to see me backstage when I was on Broadway. He had his daughter with him, and he was trying to explain the premise of *Me and My Girl* to her. "This guy, you see, in the 1930s and 1940s would have been really famous," he was saying. He only knew me as a theatre actor (I don't think Wolfie Smith had made it across the Pond) whereas he, of course, was a film star, famous all around the world. He said he couldn't understand why my performance in *Me and My Girl* was so different to another role he'd seen me play on stage. He was puzzled, he said, because American actors make themselves into a 'product'; they *become* a particular character and they market and sell that. It's why Jack Nicholson plays naughty, twinkly characters and Dustin Hoffman plays nerdy Jewish ones. They market their particular 'something'.

A few British actors, Michael Caine, Sean Connery and Hugh Grant among them, have had the nous to suss out this marketing strategy. Conversely, it's why Olivier didn't last long in Hollywood. They couldn't work him out. To me, he was the definitive actor and a complex multi-dimensional character. Others felt they couldn't pin the real Olivier down. John Lennon once tried to work with him on a project at the Royal Court, but ended up leaving for that very reason. According to Victor Spinetti, who told me this story, they had dinner at The Savoy and afterwards Lennon said, "I can't work with that guy. I don't know who he is. One minute he's this, one minute he's that. Who is he?" By the time they met, the general approach in the arts was more about being yourself, more about being true to your roots than being versatile like Olivier.

When I was at RADA it was all about versatility and adapting to the role. One day you could be skiing in a yoghurt commercial; the next you might be doing *Hamlet* on tour. I mean that's the joy of the business isn't it? I've tried to instil that in my daughter, an aspiring actress. And she's got it, as I've already mentioned – when I see her perform, she is 'different'; it's as if I am watching someone else, someone other than my daughter.

But I'm getting sidetracked; my daughter has that effect on me. So, back to New York, 1987. What I didn't know was that while Carl Reiner was following me around with his pen and paper, scripting the film that would eventually become *Bert Rigby, You're a Fool*, there was a move by Steven Spielberg to do the movie of *Me and My Girl*. Because RA wasn't there to help handle things properly, I wasn't alerted early enough to Spielberg's interest. It all became a mess. William Morris was trying to speed things up with Reiner, while I was being kept in the dark about *Me and My Girl* movie possibilities. Perhaps if I'd known in time, I could have followed the kind of career route taken by someone like Rex Harrison in *My Fair Lady*.

By this stage, all I was thinking was that I wanted to go home. Instead, I allowed the Carl Reiner thing to escalate, so that after I'd finished in *Me and My Girl* they were bringing me back over to America from England to have meetings with Lorimar Productions, the film company which was soon to be swallowed up by Warner Brothers. I was caught up with canvassing producers to get money for Carl's script, a script in which I had no real faith.

It was all motoring along, despite my best efforts at trying to delay things, when I had a call from my old agent, Felix. He'd arranged a meeting with Steven Spielberg and Andrew Lloyd Webber. I went to have tea with them at Lloyd Webber's London house in Eaton Square.

Whilst I was there, his daughter came home from school and sat eating a Chinese takeaway at the end of this thirty-seater dining table. There we were: Lloyd Webber at one end, his daughter at the other; Spielberg drinking hot water on one side of the table with his entourage, and me sitting on the other side, dying for a fag. We were listening to a recording of Sarah Brightman, Lloyd Webber's ex-wife. As I looked across at him,

Steven Spielberg was glancing quizzically at me, unsure of what to say. In the end I piped up: "Excuse me, can I ask you guys why I'm here?"

"Right, well, we're discussing work…" they said. And I asked, "Yeah, but what? Is something going to happen?" Spielberg replied: "Well, we're looking into *Me and My Girl*." Lloyd Webber came in with: "I'd just like to say that I thought you were marvellous in *Me and My Girl*." "Oh, thank you. That's very kind of you," I said, only for him to add, "You saved it from being the piece of trivia that it is." I thought that was a bit rich coming from the guy who'd given us *Starlight Express*, but let it go.

I don't think that Andrew Lloyd Webber wanted to get involved. I don't really know why he was there at all. Perhaps Spielberg was trying to work out the financial side of musicals; when Lloyd Webber told him how much he'd earned, Spielberg couldn't believe it, because he obviously thought only movies could make that kind of money. He couldn't believe that a blockbuster musical on stage could generate the same kind of cash as a film like *Jaws*.

I suppose they were also looking at the logistics of turning a musical into a film. The one idea that they came up with was *The Last Holiday*, an Alec Guinness film that they were going to 'musicalise' for the cinema. Apparently they had me in mind for the Guinness part. Whatever the case, it never happened.

Meanwhile, the wheels on *Bert Rigby* were still in motion in Hollywood, with Carl Reiner's script apparently ready and Lorimar set to produce it, having secured the money and the backing. I did a reading of the script and suddenly it was all going ahead. But instead of being excited, all I could think was 'Oh shit! I shouldn't be doing this.' But I'm sure you're used to that reaction from me by now.

It was being shot in England, so the production crew started arriving from America. One of the producers took me to Claridges for dinner, no doubt buttering me up before hitting me with: "We hate the script. We need *you* to tell Carl." "But you've given it the go ahead!" I pointed out. "Yeah, well *he's* Carl Reiner and *you're* Robert Lindsay," she pointedly said, meaning it would have more impact coming from me. We were agreed on one thing – the script wasn't ready or good enough – but we played patsy for a bit, discussing who should be the one to tell Carl. In the end it fell to me.

I had to tell Carl that his script needed a lot more work, and that this wasn't just my opinion. It didn't do any good. By now the momentum was too great. It was all going ahead, and the entire Hollywood unit had already moved to the north of England to start filming *Bert Rigby, You're a Fool*. Even the title used to make me cringe. It's an Anthony Newley-type approach to titling. The next thing I knew I was in The Dance Centre in Putney, rehearsing the script and about to start filming.

While my sense of unease about work grew, in contrast my personal life was in a really good place. I was euphoric about the arrival of Sydney, my daughter, who was born during rehearsals, and generally it was a happy time on the family and friends front. Some of this spilled over into the film. In fact, when Carl Reiner sent me a card on the film's release, he wrote, "It's the most expensive family album you'll ever have." My brother is in the film, at a football match. My mum and dad are in an audience watching me perform as Bert – there's a brilliant close-up of them right in the middle of the film as they stand up and applaud. Friends like Mike Grady are in it. Diana plays a younger version of the part played by actress Liz Smith, and even Sydney makes an appearance at the end as the baby, Kelly Astaire Rigby. Carl just brought everyone in. Anyone that knew me, he'd have in the film.

So, there I was getting the movie star treatment, taking the lead in a film that also starred Anne Bancroft and involved all these other amazing people (not least my family!). I had my own driver picking me up in a large limo from home in Chiswick and driving me off to the north of England for the filming. And they were paying me a million dollars. And yet, despite it all, deep down inside I knew that I shouldn't really be doing the film.

Oh, what a disaster! It still smarts. It still hurts. The only comforting thought was that I *knew* it was going to be a disaster. But then again, I'd been the one who thought that *Me and My Girl* was going to be a disaster! I could have written the reviews that we eventually got, right back on the day we started filming. Even so, one review in the *Daily Telegraph* still pole-axed me: "Robert Lindsay is run over by his own vehicle".

I didn't even go to the film's world premiere. I couldn't quite face it. I did go when they invited me over for a private advance screening of it in MGM Studios in Hollywood. I was sitting there in a row on my own with Carl Reiner seated somewhere behind me with the William Morris agents and one of the producers. I could hear Walter Matthau in my head, saying to Jack Lemmon in similar circumstances: "Jack, can you get out of this?" All the way through it I just kept thinking, 'Oh my God! Why did I do this?'

The screening ended and I could feel tears of despair rolling down my cheeks. "Well, Robert," said Carl. "If you didn't like that you need to see a psychiatrist!" All I could manage to say was, "Is there one available?"

They trooped down the aisle steps of the screening room, saying "Hey! You were great. This is great…" but I just knew they were being shallow and empty. They didn't mean it. It was awful. Well, I suppose, it wasn't truly terrible – there were some lovely things in it – but on the whole, it was a mess.

What it meant was that straight after the huge success, accolades and awards of *Me and My Girl* in New York came the flop of my first foray into Hollywood.

But, but, but! Let's not get too maudlin. In truth, it was probably the best thing that happened to me, ever. I suppose it's never really been documented because *Bert Rigby* has always been seen as the big 'turkey' that effectively ended my film career (interviewers don't tend to ask about it), but the truth is that by the end of *Me and My Girl* my ego had reached frightening proportions. I really did start believing my own publicity; I began to think that perhaps I was the new Fred Astaire, the new Gene Kelly, the new James Cagney. Never believe your reviews. Better still, don't read them.

So, I can't lay all the blame for my Hollywood (mis)adventure solely at the agents' door. I'd become cold and very egocentric and, in that respect, *Bert Rigby* was a fantastic lesson for me. It really knocked all that out of me and made me think, 'Hey! Stop it!' It was a wake-up call. It made me think about my life. I saw that my state of mind was contributing to the break-up with Diana, because I'd been off in never-never land, on some kind of package holiday from reality. Unfortunately, the revelation came too late for the relationship.

I can see now that the experience with *Bert Rigby* actually 'saved' me as a human being. It made me get real about myself and my acting. It was as if the part I was playing in real life had reached that moment when my 'life-script' demanded that I behave badly and get my comeuppance for so doing.

That process was further helped by the less than startling success of my next film, *Strike it Rich,* based on the book *Loser Takes All* by Graham Greene. It was a small budget film that I was asked to do with Emily Lloyd, daughter of Roger Lloyd Pack. She and I were cast as the two lovers portrayed in the rather intriguing book. Christine Oestreicher and James Scott were going to produce it, with James taking on directorial duties as well.

I met them in London when I'd just finished all the work on *Bert Rigby,* which was being edited in America, a process that would end up taking six months. During this time, Emily Lloyd was snapped up by some weird agency in LA, decided that she didn't want to do the film and then disappeared. Somewhat ridiculously, I was then sent out to Hollywood to find Emily and to persuade her to come back and do the film.

When I was there I met the 'brat pack' girls of that mid-80s era, including Demi Moore, Ally Sheedy and Molly Ringwald. Eventually Miramax, which was yet to become a major player in the film world, came into the project and insisted that Molly Ringwald do the film with me.

We began filming in France. It was a fabulous project to be involved in, with actors like John Gielgud, Max Wall, Frances De La Tour and Marius Goring taking part. Not a bad cast! A great job: twelve weeks' filming in the south of France and two thousand dollars a week. Johnny Gielgud and I became very firm friends, going to the casino what seemed like every night. One day on set, he turned to me and said, "Have you been to the Garrick recently?" I said that I hadn't, but he carried on.

"You know they've just redone the toilets. Looks very beautiful. Pale blue. Pastel colours. Makes your cock look awfully shabby!"

The next thing was the call: "Mr Gielgud. Mr Lindsay. On set please." We were doing a scene where he offers me a cigarette and I had to threaten him, but I couldn't look at him without thinking of his Garrick Club story and getting the giggles really badly. "What's the matter with you?" he asked, but I just couldn't look at him. I was sent off set for my behaviour. He was so funny, such a great man and just completely adorable.

I had a run-in with Miramax during the shooting of *Strike it Rich* when I discovered that they were still rewriting it. I was told they'd got a screenwriter in from LA to give it an overhaul, but in fact it was Harvey Weinstein, the Miramax founder himself. I caught him putting pink script pages under my hotel bedroom door one night. I opened the door and there he was, in his pyjamas, padding back toward his room. I've always liked Harvey but he can be such a bully and that certainly didn't do the film any favours. Everyone else involved in the film was frightened of him and so refused to question any of his decisions.

The long and the short of it is that *Strike it Rich* was another disaster. This failure still smarts a bit because it needn't have been like that. I can't even put my finger on quite what went wrong. What with this and the *Bert Rigby* saga, I sometimes wonder if it was all planned, scripted out as 'The Revenge of Hollywood'. Someone up there had said, "You ain't going to make it in films and it serves you right for being a pompous, arrogant little fart." Suddenly my film career in America was finished and I was back in England, looking for a job. I still maintain that it was probably the best thing that could have happened to me.

While the Hollywood experience was over, my career wasn't.

Everyone assumes that in show business you get onto the bottom rung of the ladder and start climbing up and up and that the ladder has no end. But, of course, it does. Showbiz ladders are more like stepladders anyway: you can go up and then onto a little plateau for a while, but then there's the down bit to contend with and maybe another chance to reposition and to start the climb again. Snakes and Ladders provides a better analogy: up once or twice and then down the next move you make. You try and tell young actors all this, but you can't get the message across when they are starting out. They only see the highs that they want to aim for.

After a 'down' spell, there's a bit more to it than simply 'picking yourself up, dusting yourself down and starting all over again', as per the romantic image. With acting, whatever the part, you have to ask yourself, "Why am I doing it?" And don't con yourself with the answer. Don't tell yourself you're doing a *Bert Rigby* because it's worthwhile stuff. It's the money. If I'd said to myself at the time, 'I'm doing this because I want the million dollars,' I would have been fine. That's what I learned, or rather, later realised, was the moral of it all.

Michael Caine has always said that his so-called flops still meant money in the bank, but at the time I found it hard to be so philosophical about it all. I went into such a depression that I couldn't speak to people about it – I didn't dare look at their faces. It was a horrible time.

Alan Bleasdale is the only person who's actually said, "You must have gone through hell." He said that to me on one drunken night in Manchester during the filming for *GBH*. I said: "Yeah! I did." He went on to say, "I don't know how you coped with that. You were on everyone's lips, the big conqueror of New York.

The big Tony Award winner. You were on the news. And then next thing…"

But, let it go.

41. *Me and My Girl* with Emma Thompson at the Adelphi Theatre, London.

42. We invented so much, we worked so hard and the result was magic.

43. *Me and My Girl* on Broadway. The poster
from *Hamlet* is on the wall behind me.

44. On Broadway with Michael Jackson and Quincy Jones just before I said goodnight to Bubbles. Emma Thompson sent me the trade union banner on the wall to remind me of my roots.

45. How overawed can you be? Here I am trying to look casual sitting next to Barbra Streisand while Steven Spielberg was trying to get my camera to work!

46. My first night on Broadway, with Gina Lollobrigida.

47. The day I received the Astaire Award, with Mary Tyler Moore (left) and Lynn Redgrave.

48. With Sean Connery and Maryann Plunkett, my New York leading lady. At least Sean waited until curtain down!

49. Asking Katharine Hepburn to dance. "I always wanted to dance with you." "Well, now's your chance ma'am!"

50. Portraying screen idols Charlie
Chaplin and Buster Keaton as
part of my stage act as Bert Rigby
in *Bert Rigby, You're A Fool*
directed by Carl Reiner.

51. Syd's debut in *Bert Rigby* as Kelly Astaire Rigby. I sent this photo to my daughter for her first school play with the words: "A star is born... my star. Welcome to showbiz... I love you, Dad xx".

52. Starring with Sir John Gielgud and Molly Ringwald in *Strike It Rich*. Johnny was such fun to work with.

53. In *GBH* with Julie Walters playing my mother. She has since played my lover and my wife. She will probably play my daughter next!

54. With Alan Bleasdale (left), my blood brother and my soul mate, alongside Richard Beckinsale's daughter, Samantha, who bears a remarkable likeness to her father.

55. *This is Your Life*. I wasn't best pleased about being surprised by Michael Aspel.

56. Diana was determined to get me on the show. Once I let go, the experience was a joy.

57. As Henry II in *Becket* with Derek Jacobi. Two completely different styles of acting in two great roles.

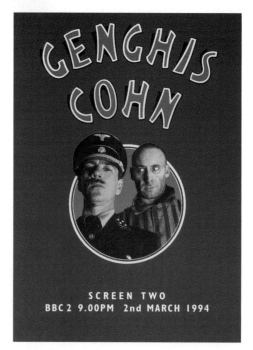

58. A promotional postcard from *Genghis Cohn*. Dressed like this, filming in Bavaria caused quite a stir!

59. In *Cyrano de Bergerac* with *that* nose.

60. *Jake's Progress* with Julie Walters and Barclay Wright. We all looked after each other and formed a strong bond. Barclay is now my godson.

61. *Brazen Hussies*. I did a strip routine in this programme. Unfortunately, it was aired when I was sitting in A & E at a hospital. My fellow patients looked very bemused!

62. This is how I wanted Richard III to look…

63. …and this is how
I chose to play him.

64. Always the joker! Merry
Christmas Mr Billington…

65. On the set of *Fierce Creatures*. This is how I met Princess Diana… well, my daughter Syd approved!

66. *Hornblower* was another opportunity to spend time with my beloved daughter.

67. *Oliver!* at the Palladium. A bomb scare once stopped the production and we were all ushered into the street in our costumes. I was even offered a free copy of the *Big Issue!*

68. Lionel Bart supported my decision to use the nose to play Fagin in *Oliver!* But what a make-up job every night.

69. This picture of my TV Fagin in *Oliver Twist* appeared in a local paper. Our butcher saw it and said to Dad, "Your son gets more and more like you every day"!

70. Playing Archie Rice in *The Entertainer.*

71. As Michael Jericho in *Jericho*. Recreating the Fifties stirred so many memories.

72. Beside Uncle Cyril's grave near Florence. It's strange to visit a family member's resting place so far from home.

73. With Phoebe Nicholls as Cherie in *The Trial of Tony Blair*.
"Drop the impression and play the man," said the director.

74. David Aukin persuaded me to play the megalomaniac Onassis in *Aristo* at
the Minerva in Chichester, with Elizabeth McGovern as Jackie Kennedy.

75. I thought I was playing Onassis,
in fact I was playing my father.

76. Me with Dad in Los Angeles.

77. My mini Aristos! Sam (left) and Jamie.

78.
With Zoë Wanamaker at the TV Quick and TV Choice Awards 2007 where *My Family* won Best Comedy Show – one of numerous awards for the programme which has a following of millions.

79. With Rosie, Syd and Sam.

My real family – the age gap between my daughter and two sons is exactly the same as the gap between me and my brother and sister. Life goes in cycles…

80. With Rosie, Sam and Jamie (front).

81. Sorry, where was I? My daughter always has that effect on me.

SIXTEEN

MILITANT TENDENCIES

I'VE NEVER really had a career plan. When I left school, the best that anyone had said about me was that I had the gift of the gab, and that evaluation came from my woodwork teacher! Hardly a glowing endorsement with which to step forth into the working world.

I *had* done local amateur and school plays, causing a bit of a stir in the process, and, of course, there was that speech from *Henry V* on the school stage that gave me some confidence. But all I had really was this basic desire to perform. And, as things have turned out, that's really all that I've done ever since.

But have I had a life plan? No. I subscribe more to the Disraeli quote given to me by Alan Bleasdale in one of his faxes (he doesn't do e-mail!): 'Youth is a blunder; Manhood a struggle; Old Age a regret'. Perhaps that's why it feels like my career has always had its moments of turmoil.

Whenever I talk with Alan I always realise how much I've missed him. When we last spoke, he was just about to finish a big project he'd been working away at and he was going on about TV executives and how the business has changed. I've always called him a blood brother (and no, I don't confuse him with Willy Russell!) because he manages to say the things I want to say. I think he's a genius. He's passionate. He's caring. He's a mess. He's insecure. He's just wonderful. One lovely thing he says is that he's never met a perfect human being, and that if you do meet one or you think you've met one, don't you just mistrust them? This is why he makes his writing so honest and why, I think, it is identifiable to such a big audience.

Jake's Progress, written by Alan for Channel Four in the early 1990s, is one of the best things I've ever done. I know *GBH* (the earlier Bleasdale series on which I worked) won all the awards, but *Jake's Progress* is a monumental piece of work, a powerful dissection of relationships and marriage. As the series director Robin Lefevre said during the reading for *Jake's Progress*, it's a modern Greek tragedy.

It's about this couple, played by Julie Walters and myself, who have a perfect, totally happy marriage blessed with a wonderful child, Jake. Then the wife starts to get suspicious that her husband might be having an affair. But although he is attractive to women because he is a friendly man and a good dad who takes his son to school, he has no inclination to be unfaithful. He hasn't strayed.

The wife then does the most provocative thing: she asks a clairvoyant to read her husband's palm and tell him that he's going to have an affair. After a while, the information starts to haunt him. If someone tells you what you're going to do, you begin to think it's going to happen and, in some weird way, it can be *made* to happen – I suppose it's the power of suggestion. And that was their downfall, because then, of course, he *does* have an affair. The end, when the cheating couple fall off the cliff to protect Jake, who ends up falling too, is pure Greek tragedy. A wonderful, wonderful piece. Great vision.

Alan celebrates what most people call 'ordinary' life, because he believes that actually there is no such thing as ordinary. It's a quality that always appears in Julie's work too, which is why it's so monumental and why I admire it so much. When I started out in acting, I always wanted to play the kings or the popes or the Gods, but what Alan and Julie have both taught me is that the 'great' ones are the ones like you and me. They made me realise that there's a 'king' inside us; that we're all capable of greatness.

When I did a BAFTA tribute for Julie, I said that she loves the characters she plays. Not just that – she understands them because she comes from amongst the people. She used to work as a nurse in a senility ward and I remember she was *always* telling stories about the things that happened there. Even though people were going loopy and crying, sometimes dying, it was the celebration of life that she remembered. She told me that every old man that was about to die suddenly missed his mother. In their eighties and nineties, they still wanted their mum. When Julie told you stories, she always enriched them with wonderful observations about people.

Meeting Alan has been very important to me both in my work and as a person. When I started working with him, and with Julie, I realised almost straight away that I had a lot to celebrate about where I came from. I didn't have to be embarrassed about my roots. I could celebrate my background and what I would call my 'ordinariness'. It's a cliché I know, but there is no such thing as ordinary. We are all extraordinary. All of us.

Working with Alan came after my brief flirtation with Hollywood, that fickle mistress, had ended. I felt as if I had come home.

There were a couple of false starts with Alan before we actually got to meet. Our first near miss came many years ago, when I was still living with Diana. Julie phoned me up in the early hours of the morning when, strangely enough, I was still awake. I didn't really know her back then, although we'd met once at a party or something, very briefly. "Hi Bob! It's Julie. I've got Alan with me. Can you come out and meet him. He's dying to meet you." I pointed out that it was two o'clock in the morning. "Oh is it? Oh… well can we swap numbers… you need to get together with Alan 'cos he really wants to meet you. We've been talking about you all evening." Actually, I wanted to get straight over there and meet them right there and then, but I didn't. Alan was already well known through *Boys from the Blackstuff*; he had this reputation as a working-class poet of a writer. But then I heard no more. That was it.

The second 'nearly' moment came when I arrived back from America, tail between my legs after the *Bert Rigby/Strike it Rich* saga. I was staying at the Midland Hotel in Manchester, helping to set up a production of *The Count of Monte Cristo* at the Royal Exchange whilst also filming an ill-fated series for Granada called *Confessional*. Braham Murray was pushing me to do the stage show but my heart wasn't really in it. However, news of the show had gone public, so Alan knew, having written *GBH* with me in mind, that he'd 'lost' me. Verity Lambert, the producer, rang him and said, "He's booked. He can't do it."

Alan, being Alan, sent the *GBH* scripts to me at the Midland Hotel anyway, with a note saying something like 'If you don't do this, you're insane: we have to work together'. I started to work my way though this mountain of paper (it was a seven-part series) and just read and read. I went into the night, totally hooked, reading this huge script. By the end I just thought, 'I've got to do this.' It's the story of Michael Murray, a power-mad, corrupt councillor who finds himself at war with Jim Nelson, a schoolteacher who inadvertently defies a twenty-four-hour strike organised by Murray. As the two elements clash, their lives begin to unravel. It was Alan's thinly veiled response to events that took place in Liverpool in the 1980s, when the left-wing Militant Tendency took charge of the city council.

So, I pulled out of *The Count of Monte Cristo,* which almost landed me in litigation with the Royal Exchange. Braham Murray was up for suing me. Fortunately, although it all got a bit nasty, it didn't quite reach the point where lawyers were called in. I had to pretend that I just didn't want to do the production, even though the real reason I was walking away was because I wanted to do *GBH*.

Thank God I did. It changed my whole outlook on the business. After *Bert Rigby* my world was on the floor: I was shattered; my self-esteem had completely gone. But *GBH* gave me that self-esteem back – it proved to me that I could still act.

The series became an instant classic, and did really well at the BAFTAs in 1992. I won the BAFTA for Best Actor and suddenly I was top 'kiddie' again, all thanks to Alan.

The whole experience on *GBH* was amazing. Although the Michael Murray part was written for me, they gave it to Michael Palin when I wasn't initially available. Alan then had to ring Michael to say that Bob was now able to take the part. Fortunately Michael said, "Well he's got to do Michael Murray. I can play Jim." How generous of him!

I do think the Ancient Greeks had a point. There is such a

thing as destiny. There are Gods that decide on certain things. I'd had a terrible 'dip'. I was completely lost from a career point of view; I was thinking of giving the whole thing up. And then one hit production just turned everything around. That's how the business is. Of course, it wasn't all about the Gods – a couple of mortals helped out too: it was thanks to Alan's persistence and Michael's generosity that I was able to benefit from playing Michael Murray.

Actually, I think Michael Palin would have made a very good Michael Murray, but clearly he wasn't exactly what Alan wanted when he wrote the part with me in mind. Alan knew there was a 'side' to me. He used to watch me in *Citizen Smith* and *Get Some In*, both sitcoms, and yet saw something serious and dark there. How about that for observation? I'd been Jack the Lad, a cockney boy, in both of those programmes and yet the part Alan wrote for me was a Scouse politician with a very, very dark past; an extremely haunted man on the edge of a nervous breakdown.

Alan had recognised my insecurities and, as I've already pointed out, was the only one who approached me after *Bert Rigby* to say that I must have gone through hell. It was only when someone like Alan said that to me that I realised how awful it had been, and that I'd been trying to hide that sense of failure from people. It's ghastly when you're 'up there' in a place like New York, to be wanted by everybody one minute and then rejected the next, to be leaving with no one speaking to you at all. Only two years after I'd won a Tony Award and been feted, I was reading dreadful reviews and making my own way to the airport by taxi (the chauffeur was long gone) to leave the US.

The great *GBH* script allowed me to get back on the horse

after my nasty fall from 'grace'. It gave me the chance to explore character, to create a complex individual who gradually loses his grip. While Alan had written this knockout script, I also got the chance to invent, to add my own quirks to the character. One element I was keen to develop was the use of individual mannerisms to reflect inner turmoil. Alan had written in the famous Michael Murray twitch and it was my job to make it as real as possible, but it was something that was nearly removed altogether from the final performance by a cabal of writer, director and commissioning editor.

They confronted me saying they wanted me to drop the nervous tic. Apparently they were very worried about it, but I'd already 'set' it with the continuity girl. "Everything I do, you must monitor," I explained to her, adding that she had to let me know what part of the film we were in. This was important because we shot out of sequence, filming the end quite early on in production. I knew that the story culminated in a nervous breakdown for Michael Murray, but the physical signals of this psychosis had to build gradually, intensifying to the point where he was completely out of control. So, the twitch had to start off with a wink – and the audience must think it is *only* a wink.

One day during filming in a school playground, I found myself faced with Robert Young – the director, Alan Bleasdale – the writer and Peter Ansorge – the commissioning editor. "Robert, we're getting a bit worried about the twitch," they said. "We think we might have to cut it." "Over my dead body," I replied. "No honestly, Bob," said Robert Young, taking the lead. "It's just that we don't think it's rooted in any reality. We think it might be a bit over the top; we're worried it's going to ruin your performance. People don't have these sorts of tics."

I stood there studying them while they were explaining all this to me. Robert Young was standing on one leg while he was talking because he was so nervous. There he was, standing on one leg and holding the other one up, clutching his foot to his backside like a security blanket. Alan Bleasdale stood beside him, his arm up in the air as if he was holding up the sky. Finally there was Peter Ansorge, absentmindedly stood with his hand down the front of his trousers.

I was staring at the three of them, fixedly looking at each one. "So you lot think it's over the top do you?" I asked. "People don't have these kind of tics? Just look at the three of you!" They looked at each other, smiled and conceded: "It's in, it's in... OK... absolutely."

GBH was originally meant to be three ninety-minute episodes, but Alan can't stop writing. This is his big problem. What he needs is a good producer like Verity Lambert, who tried to rein him in on *GBH*, and a strong woman like his wife, Julie, to keep him on track and focused. When Julie is away, he goes to pieces. The length of the episodes for *GBH* ended up being rather uneven. The first was ninety minutes, the second was fifty minutes and then the five remaining episodes all had different running times.

After *Boys from the Blackstuff*, I suppose, he had carte blanche to do whatever he wanted. Company networks would ring him up and say, "Give us anything and we'll do it." Unfortunately they can't afford to do that now. I once said to him: "Alan it's economics. You can't just write willy-nilly. Things have changed – you have to write to order these days." Not so long ago ITV, for example, cut £180 million pounds from its drama budget. The trend toward frugality in TV just isn't conducive to quality drama of the sort produced by Alan. It was fortunate that

GBH was made when it was and that Alan was able to do it largely the way that he wanted to.

The series was an immediate success. I was on holiday in Cornwall with Diana when it went out on TV. She phoned me from the nearby village the next morning, having gone out for supplies, and told me I was all over the front pages of the newspapers. I just about managed a wary "What?" I couldn't believe it. There were photos of me playing Michael Murray alongside pictures of Labour leader Neil Kinnock and the infamous deputy leader of Liverpool City Council, Derek Hatton, on whom *GBH* was said to be loosely based. I spent the rest of the day taking calls from the press.

"Well done. You're back. You've done it," said Diana, who'd had to live with the post-*Me and My Girl* trials and tribulations.

I don't know if the Kinnocks in particular took enjoyment from the demise of the militant Michael Murray in *GBH*, but not long after the programme went out they seemed keen to befriend us. It was during the run up to the 1992 General Election. They invited Diana and me, along with Alan and Julie, to The Ivy one night. Suddenly we were seen everywhere with them. It was the most bizarre thing. When I was doing *Becket*, Neil Kinnock would come backstage and say, "We're taking you out for dinner tonight." There I was with the scourge of the Militant Tendency, the man who was being groomed to be the next prime minister.

I've never been that active politically (remember, all that Wolfie Smith stuff was me acting!), but during the *GBH* period I got drawn into that world by the series' subject matter. It all spilled over into the BAFTAs. On the night, before proceedings started, four of the seven judges, who we all knew and who were independent producers, came over to our table and basically said, "Congratulations, *GBH* has won. I voted for you." The evening wore on. I got up and received Best Actor. Elvis Costello won Best Music for *GBH* and... here we go..."the winner of the Best Drama Series is... *Prime Suspect*". There was a gasp. Alan, who was a bit drunk by that point, got up, stormed over to one of the judges and said, "Fookin' 'ell! You said you'd voted for me!" "I did, I did!" he said. It turned out that the voting slips had disappeared, so there was no way of confirming how the judges had voted.

Maybe politics took the BAFTA away from us that night. There was no way that we were going to be allowed to be at the Kinnocks' table, celebrating the BAFTA for Best Drama Series, as well as the supposed demise of the extreme left. It wasn't simply a case of sour grapes on our part: after the ceremony, four of the seven voting jury members signed a public statement declaring they'd voted for *GBH*. It became known as BAFTA-gate. I was going to send my gong back, but Alan persuaded me not to, telling me I'd won it for my acting, that it was nothing to do with politics. True enough, but they ought to have given him something too.

He and Verity ended up suing the *Evening Standard*, whose TV critic had described Alan's reaction as paranoia. It turned out that the critic had been one of the judges and had voted against *GBH* and for *Prime Suspect*. Alan and Verity won a lump sum but the whole affair left a very sour taste in the mouth. It made me realise how much we're all manipulated.

SEVENTEEN

TWO GO MAD IN IRELAND

THE NEXT 'Bleasdale' (which was what people used to ask, as in, 'what's the next Bleasdale going to be?') was *Jake's Progress*, which meant filming in Ireland for seven and a half months, right down in the south, in County Waterford. Again, Alan had written it for me – or rather with me in mind.

Jake's Progress unfolded against the backdrop of my break-up with Diana Weston, a split made much more painful by the fact that we had our daughter, Sydney, to worry about. It was a really difficult time. I was all right initially, but as things broke down between Diana and me it got worse and worse. I moved out of the house and took a flat in Chelsea Harbour. Because I was going backwards and forwards between London and Ireland, I was only seeing Syd for odd weekends and it became very distressing.

When Syd came out to Ireland with Diana at half term, Alan and the director, Robin Lefevre, tried to keep Diana and I together. They meant well but it was too late – things had become really messy, particularly as the press was involved which always complicates matters.

My off-set crisis found an unnerving parallel in the story of *Jake's Progress*, with its depiction of a relationship breakdown. On occasions it was too near the knuckle. Unlike *GBH*, we shot *Jake's Progress* in sequence, and as my real life seemed to be falling apart, so the character in *Jake's Progress* was matching me step for step. The pressure of living that scenario twenty-four hours a day, on set and off, was awful, and in the end I had a minor nervous breakdown. It started one morning when I'd drunk too much the night before. Everyone had gone off for the weekend, back to their homes, and I realised that I didn't have one. I was really down and depressed, and contemplating overdoses and all sorts of things. They were dark times – I really was in danger of going over the edge. That's probably why I feel far more personally connected to *Jake's Progress* than many other things I've done. I can't watch it anymore. Some friends of mine wanted to dig out the DVD recently and to watch it with me, but I just couldn't face it.

I wasn't really able to talk in depth with Alan during the filming. At a time like that, when he's working, it's very difficult to draw his attention away because he's totally and completely preoccupied with the project in hand. I think he knew I was going through torment and turmoil, but he really couldn't get too involved. He's got the stress of filming and, to be fair, has employed me to do a job of work and doesn't need me having a nervous breakdown on set. In the end I dealt with it on my own and was quite proud that I did.

I don't think I am alone in this profession in struggling to cope when it seems like your own life is as riddled with angst as your character's. You have to have a safety valve to deal with it. It's this 'technique' thing again, of being the character and inhabiting the character, but being able to leave it behind, separate from your own life. If you can't do that, you can easily go right over the edge.

My best work, for which I've received most praise, has always come when the character has gone back in the drawer at night. They're usually characters that I feel I really know and that are 'near' to me, but that I can leave behind at the end of the day's filming. It is difficult to explain, but it's best for the part (and for yourself) if you can avoid being taken over by it, if you can just drop in and out when required.

The split with Diana was traumatic but I think the aftermath could have turned out far worse than it did. Indeed, the way it was handled by all concerned demonstrates that a relationship break-up need not destroy your lives or those of your children. Diana and I have managed to nurture a special friendship out of a failed relationship, and for that I'm grateful – not least as it means we possess a beautiful, gifted and well-adjusted daughter.

I wasn't the only one on *Jake's Progress* trying to contend with a personal crisis. Julie Walters was suffering the torment of her daughter being very ill and Barclay Wright, who played our son Jake, had to deal with huge problems in his own life, some of which mirrored what was happening in the script. A special bond of mutual support was created during the filming, which helped us all to get through seven months of being cut off from our families in deepest Ireland. Julie was great company during a period when I felt desperately lonely and, I'm pleased to say, it's a friendship that has lasted. We held each other up at a difficult time and I hope that we also helped shield Barclay from the harsh realities of his personal life.

213

Some of the filming took place in Ardmore Studios just south of Dublin – the only studio that I know with a tin roof. It does rain a lot in Ireland, so I'll leave you to draw your own conclusions from a sound recording point of view. We all stayed in a nearby hotel that had more than a passing resemblance to Fawlty Towers. Oh God! That hotel! You couldn't really stay there for any length of time without falling back on a sense of humour. It was in the middle of a council estate but had this solitary, sorry-looking turret which I'm sure was made of plastic or something. The Americans, for some bizarre reason, went there in their droves, mainly I think because the Irish told them that one of the wings was haunted.

I could have told them what it was haunted by: workmen and music. The hotel played music constantly, piping it into all the rooms, driving us crazy. And then there were the workmen – it seemed like they were piped into every room too. Julie and I had adjoining rooms, and because the car came to collect us both at some unearthly hour, we'd usually be taking our morning shower at about the same time – we knew this because we could talk to each other through the paper-thin wall.

One morning we were both singing away in the shower when this voice piped up in a strong Irish accent: "Hello! Hello! Is the water coming through alright?" Well, actually, no, it had suddenly stopped. On most mornings the water would fluctuate between hot and cold but, on this particular day, it stopped altogether. I heard Julie go, "Oh shit!" and then the Irish voice again: "Sorry about this. The water will be coming through in a minute."

"Who's that?" I said. "It's the plumber. I'm fixing the pipes." "Well, that's great, but we're late for work. Could you put the water back on please?" Julie said later that what was so funny about it was that we were both talking to the showerhead because this plumber was above us.

The voice came in again: "Hello! Is that Julie Walters?" She said, "Yes, who's that?" "Oh, I'm sorry Miss Walters. I'm not looking. I'm not looking, I promise. I know it's you staying with us." And then the water magically reappeared, although it was so hot I had to get out straight away. Now *that* was a typical morning at the hotel.

The evenings weren't much better. When my agent, the wonderful Steve Kenis from the English arm of William Morris, tried to ring me up at the hotel, he asked if he could please speak to Robert Lindsay. An Irish voice greeted him with: "Oh yes, certainly I'll put you through to the bar." "Right, thank you very much." "Hello," this time from the bar. "Yes, can I speak to Robert Lindsay please?" "Oh yes, I'll just put you through to the kitchen." "What? Hello, yes, could I speak to Robert Lindsay?" "Oh yes, I'll just put you through to the hall." By now frustrated, Steve says, "Excuse me, I'm looking for Robert Lindsay," and the soothing Irish lilt replies, "Oh right, *Robert* Lindsay. I thought you were talking about the manager." "Oh, I see, your manager is called Mr Lindsay?" asks the agent, not unreasonably. "Oh no! He's called Michael Malone."

I'm pretty sure the mischievous Irish sense of humour often had as much to do with the misunderstandings as any breakdown in communications. They enjoyed sending up the important acting types from across the water – and why not! Filming on location one day we decided to book a table at the local fish restaurant that evening. It was a place right on a cliff edge. Alan thought it would be ideal for a company gathering. So I rang up the restaurant during the lunch break. "Hello, could I make a reservation for tonight?" The answer came back in a strong Irish accent: "Hello, who's speaking?" "It's Robert Lindsay here." "Oh! Robert. How's the filming going? I've been watching you from the restaurant and it looks amazing what you're doing there. It looks very exciting." I said, "Well actually we're going to come for dinner tonight if that's alright." The voice now sounds a little concerned: "Oh! Right, right. Well I'm afraid I don't take reservations." "Right. OK." Then he said, "Well how many are there?" "There'll be about twelve, maybe fifteen." He said, "Oh! Right. What time you comin'?" "About eight o'clock," I replied. "I'll tell you what. I'll save you a table…"

On most weekends, when the filming (and circuitous conversations with the locals) tended to stop, Julie and I would fly back to the UK together. We'd leave Ireland on a Friday night, with Julie insisting on watching the end of *Coronation Street* in the airport lounge before catching our flight. They'd even call out for her at Cork Airport with, "Miss Walters, has the programme finished yet?"

It was a real schlep from County Waterford, a two-and-a-half hour drive on a Friday night to catch the last flight back to London. Sometimes we missed it. I found that very hard – it was the first time that I'd only been able to see my daughter at weekends and it was really important that I got back. I used to get incredibly frustrated if the director asked for another shot. Because they were all staying, it didn't matter to them, but Julie and I had to get back – me to Syd and Julie to her daughter – so we would both be beside ourselves.

It was always a very odd weekend: Friday night, back to Heathrow Airport; pick up Syd from Chiswick; a weekend at Chelsea Harbour; fly back to Ireland on Sunday night. That was the routine for almost eight months. Despite all the stress involved, *Jake's Progress* remains one of my career highs. It was an extraordinary piece of work at what was an extraordinary time for me.

Jake's Progress said more to me about relationships (and how they break up) than any other piece of work I've been in or seen. My character in the series had become a househusband; his wife was to be the one out earning money. Alan explored how this change in roles affected the marital relationship. He illustrated the pressures that families face when that work balance shifts, creating a scenario that put me in mind of all those northern towns where the factories and mines have closed, and the effect that it's had on men in the north. Alan was trying to examine this turnaround, the dramatic change that emerged from the whole Thatcher movement in the 1980s. A lot of guys just hadn't been able to cope with it and that's what *Jake's Progress* is all about.

I notice it now in Ilkeston, my home town. Men have lost their identity, whilst the women have gone onto further education and are working in or running companies. By contrast, the blokes don't seem to know what they are doing or where they're going.

My 'Bleasdales' continued with *Oliver Twist* for TV after a gap of about four years during which, amongst other things, I did *Richard III* at The Haymarket and, coincidentally, the musical *Oliver!* at the Palladium. I played Fagin in the TV adaptation, but the series ended up being a rather hit-and-miss affair. Alan went more off-track than ever before with the story, and perhaps he should have been controlled a bit more. I think the key problem was the idea to do the back-story. It meant great parts for Marc Warren and Lindsay Duncan, but the audience couldn't quite get their heads round it, particularly in America. "It's *Oliver*

Twist," they cried, "and we didn't get to meet Oliver for two whole episodes." It was a shame because I was rather proud of it overall and for what I did as Fagin, particularly the scene in the jail when he's about to be hanged. It's a scene that's in the book, but rarely makes it into a screen adaptation.

I miss working with Alan. Looking back, it seems as if I've had several 'Road to Damascus' moments but Alan was the person who led me back to my roots. He reminded me that I didn't have to run away from my past or blame anyone for the things that happened to me. He has stayed true to his roots, steadfastly refusing to leave his beloved Liverpool, and taught me to be proud of my heritage and my upbringing. Alan also cares very much for the people he writes about and I love the fact that he writes everything with an actor in mind. You might not always take the part in the end, but he has you in his head when he's writing. He even puts your picture up on the wall. My problem is that the only picture he's got of me is twenty years old!

Alan isn't an angry man by any means but he is passionately against corruption and, to quote Hamlet, he is unable to "bear the whips and scorns of time, the oppressor's wrong... the Law's delay, the insolence of office..."

I was talking to him recently about the parallel between football and the entertainment industry, between sport on the one hand and film and TV on the other. They're both run by people who don't really have a passion for their chosen field. To them it is a business. They are in it for themselves and the position and esteem it gives them. They are the men in suits. Everyone you meet at the top end of football now is running a corporate enterprise.

It is the same in film and TV. I tried to capture this at Sir Bill

Cotton's memorial service in February 2009, including these few words about men in suits in my tribute to him: "Creative people – writers, actors, directors – have a fear of men in suits. Men in suits represent, to creative people, the abyss between creativity and money. Well, Bill always wore a suit. He came from a generation that was born in a suit. But underneath that suit he wore a swimsuit, a clown's outfit, a tutu… a song and dance outfit. He was a man of many parts."

Apart from the odd, notable exception, I work in an unforgiving business that leaves creative people feeling incredibly vulnerable. That's certainly the way it is if you're an actor – unless you've got an ego the size of a house, you can't help but feel insecure. The story of my old friend John Normington shows how bad it can be.

I was woken early one morning in late 2007 by a call from John's partner, also called John, an American make-up artist and wig maker. John and John had lived together for forty years and recently become civil partners. I'd worked with partner John on *Cyrano de Bergerac* and had been working with actor John in *The Entertainer*. Partner John was calling to tell me the very sad news of actor John's death.

John Normington had been playing my father, Billy Rice, in the play, but was taken *really* ill during the run and had to leave the show after about three weeks. What we didn't know was that he had been suffering from pancreatic cancer. *He* knew that. *He* knew he was dying.

The tragedy is that he wouldn't tell anyone, because he didn't want it to get round the business. That happens to a lot of actors. They get ill and they don't tell anyone. The simple truth is that if people know you're ill, they don't employ you. Even if you get better, if they know you've been ill they won't employ you. You're a liability. You can't be insured.

It seems the ultimate irony to me that you spend your whole life acting and, even when you're dying, you still have to act – you have to pretend that everything is OK. This profession is cruel right up to the last minute and people should be aware of that when they come into it.

EIGHTEEN

PET HATES

AFTER FILMING *Jake's Progress* I entered a rather weird period of work. I did *The Wimbledon Poisoner* for TV with Robert Young, who'd also directed *GBH*. It came out as an absolute pig's ear. It was an extremely funny book but the problem was that Nigel Williams, author of the novel and a wonderfully witty writer, also wrote the screenplay. It is perhaps an object lesson for all authors: at some point, you have to let go.

Not long afterwards, in 1997, I got a part in the John Cleese film *Fierce Creatures*. Everyone was telling me I shouldn't do it, but I thought it fitted in with the new life I was trying to carve out for myself, taking jobs that allowed me to balance work with seeing my daughter as much as I could. I just thought: Pinewood, Syd, animals – sounds good – I'll be close to home, have weekends off and it will be lots of fun for my animal-loving daughter. That worked out to be the case and Syd often came on set during the filming.

However, the film turned out to be… let's just say 'good in parts' is a fair assessment. It didn't help that it had two directors with Fred Schepisi coming in to direct it after Robert Young.

With *Fierce Creatures* I realised again the power of America, or the men in tracksuits, when it came to making movies. Jamie Lee Curtis and Kevin Kline, who are both fantastic people, had tough American lawyers and agents around them throughout the shoot and were able to dictate changes to their benefit and to our detriment.

There was a whole gang of us who were playing the zookeepers in the film. Originally, they were really funny parts, but we'd come in every morning and discover that another section of the script had been chopped or rewritten. One of the extra writers came clean one day. "Actually, Jamie's agents are insisting it's rewritten," they revealed. My part, Sydney Lotterby, started out as the fourth biggest in the film but that certainly wasn't how he finished up.

The basic gag was that we all had to be like the animals we were in charge of. We all had to *be* our animals. I was a rodent. A coatimundi to be precise. I had two big front teeth, a tangle of hair and a beard. My character was passionate about his animals, saying "Eh you can't do this to our animals" and suchlike. It was very funny, or at least it was until they started cutting out the animal-related stuff. We were all doing different animals and so went off to research how they behaved: Michael Palin was doing bats and Ronnie Corbett was supposed to be the sea-lion keeper. Ronnie spent weeks at London Zoo, learning all about this creature's behaviour so that he would look like he knew what he was doing. All of that went out of the window once they began changing the script. We were left looking like complete lunatics. There were whole scenes where they've got the best character actors around and they're all stood there doing nothing.

For all that, there were a few highlights. We were shooting one scene in which Kevin Kline makes a major speech. The rest of us had to stand with our backs to the camera and then, on cue, all turn around at once. The director said, "As you turn, I say 'Action' and then I'm going to show you something that will help achieve the right tone for the scene." So we all turned round, and there, stood in front of us, were Princess Diana and Prince William. They were just back from a holiday in Greece, looking very tanned and glam. She had her white jeans on, and they both wore pale blue shirts. Our jaws hit the floor; one of the extras even fainted with the excitement.

I was standing there as Sydney Lotterby, zookeeper, made up to look like Hoover the coatimundi. "Hello, nice to meet you Princess Diana," I managed, thinking to myself, '*This* is what I do for a living!'

We had the odd visit from Hollywood royalty too. Tom Cruise regularly came down to Pinewood to show his children the animals. It was better than taking them to the zoo as there were leopards, tigers, polar bears and loads of others animals, as well as tanks full of reptiles and fish. The whole backlot was just a menagerie of *Fierce Creatures*.

So, the coatimundi. I know you're wondering. I'll put you out of your misery – it's like a South American badger, a very powerful creature that looks rather like a wombat with a long nose. I had to do two weeks of training with the creature to prepare for the role, but I never liked the little bastard. They're really strong animals and I knew that at various times during the shoot I was required to hold this thing. Its keeper and trainer, this Russian guy, said, "Hoover is sooo friendly. You get heem and you hug heem... he likes hugging..." So I go to 'hug heem' and 'kiss heem' and he just bites my face. Little sod. I was rushed off to Pinewood's medical centre for a tetanus jab with blood pouring down my cheek. So that was my first introduction to Hoover.

There was a definite feeling of mutiny in the air from the zookeepers. Our roles had been pared down from major parts to what were little more than extras and I began to wonder why on earth I was doing the film. I wasn't the only one thinking that way and the usually mild-mannered Ronnie Corbett was the first to crack. He came up to me one day on set and said (and here a refined Edinburgh accent and the impeccable timing of Mr Corbett wouldn't go amiss): "Do you realise that these animals are being treated better than us? Look at that leopard, just look at it, sneering at us. We're being treated like animals while *they*," he whispered, "are probably getting paid more than all of us put together."

It was probably a mad idea to write a whole film about animals, and even madder to get all these actors together in one scene with their animals: me, Jack Davenport, his mother Maria Aitken, Lisa Hogan, Ronnie Corbett, Derek Griffiths, Carey Lowell and Michael Palin, all walking into a room with our animals, hoping they didn't rip each other, or us, to pieces. A word of advice, in case you ever find yourself in that situation – keep the llama away from the South American coatimundi. We were each doing what we needed to be doing at the camera, but the animals were doing something completely different. It was total chaos. At one point Ronnie just disappeared out of shot. Had the leopard finally got him?

It was another 'great' movie experience for me, one to add to the others! American movies often rewrite history and play around with facts as if they don't care. I went up for – but didn't get – *101 Dalmatians* after doing *Fierce Creatures*. I remember seeing the script and thinking, 'Why is there a raccoon in this?' At a script reading I mentioned that you didn't get too many raccoons in England. "Oh, it doesn't matter," I was told. "But *101 Dalmatians* is an English story," I said. "It's based in Gloucestershire!" They told me people don't care about things like that. I tried to tell them that children would care, but I didn't get very far. They kept the raccoon in the film and kept *me* out of it.

Not long after finishing *Fierce Creatures*, two new film scripts landed on my PA's desk. One was *Lock, Stock and Two Smoking Barrels*, the other was *Divorcing Jack*. I picked up *Divorcing Jack* first. Mine was to be a part playing the Irish Prime Minister. 'Oh yeah, Belfast,' I thought. 'Filming in Belfast. I'll do that.' I didn't even read *Lock Stock*. More's the pity – it just goes to show how important those casual decisions can be.

Divorcing Jack went straight to video, whereas *Lock Stock and Two Smoking Barrels*, as you probably know, was a major success. *Divorcing Jack* was based on a very good book by Colin Bateman but, again, it didn't transfer so well to the screen. I played a former IRA killer and worked really hard to learn the Northern Irish accent. Everyone else was authentic too – the accents worked. Then, after the film was completed, the producers and director said, "Oh, but you see, he should have a slightly American accent, because he'd lived in America." Great. Now you tell me.

The truth is they wanted to Americanise the film for the US market. And that meant they had to re-dub the entire film. I had to go back through it and dub the new, slightly amended accent over each scene. As a lead, I had lots of speech in close-up and so it was a nightmare. The film actually released to great reviews: the critics loved it, even if the public didn't. But, there was a bad mention for me somewhere – it said something like: 'Robert Lindsay... the worst attempt at a Northern Irish accent ever'.

Sod's law isn't it? If only I'd read that bloody Guy Ritchie script.

NINETEEN

EIGHT MILES FROM ACTON

AFTER BEING reunited with Julie Walters on *Brazen Hussies,* a rather surreal but very good Elijah Moshinsky TV piece in which everything seemed to be coloured pink, I went to shoot *Goodbye My Love* in Tennessee for Granada Films in the autumn of 1996.

Experiencing the Fall in Tennessee was just extraordinary. I'd never seen anything quite as beautiful, the colours so vibrant and so red it looked like the place was on fire. However, beyond the visual treats of nature, Tennessee felt like a strange place. It was a weird piece too. I was playing Derek Humphry, a real guy, who'd written *Final Exit*, a book that dealt with euthanasia. The filming didn't come long after the break-up with Diana, so I wasn't feeling at my most secure, and perhaps playing a character that was advocating euthanasia wasn't a good thing to be doing at a time like that. I certainly didn't feel at ease.

Over in the States, Derek Humphry has a rather fanatical following, and some of his 'cult' visited us on set. They wanted to find out what I was doing, why I was doing it and what the script was about. It was all really spooky. Some of them even posed as extras to get on set.

I'd experienced that kind of 'infiltration' before, on *GBH*. Michael Palin and I were in a school classroom (Michael's character was a schoolteacher, so most of the scenes between us were filmed in a school), larking around one day, waiting to go on set and reminiscing about things. The extras were sitting around and one of them, a real Scouser, came up and said, "Hello Michael, I'm playing the… erm. What's the script about? What you playin'?" Michael said, "I play a schoolteacher." Having engaged Michael's attention, he asked, "Is it based on Derek Hatton?" "Well, yeah sort of, loosely," responded Michael. I was looking at Michael's face and mouthing, "Shut up." He suddenly realises too and clams up. We asked the director Robert Young who the two new extras were. "Well I don't know," he said. "I didn't employ them. I'll ask the First."

They weren't on the First's list – he didn't know who they were either. It turned out they were Derek Hatton's 'representatives', sent to find out what the script was about. It was then that I began to realise just how brilliant and powerful *GBH* was going to be, because it focused so cleverly on intimidation and that whole militant left thing. It was fascinating stuff.

After that experience, being infiltrated by the 'cult' people posing as extras on *Goodbye My Love* didn't come as a particular surprise. You might think that this type of thing doesn't happen, that individuals wouldn't bother to go to such lengths, but it does and they do. Security can become an issue in those circumstances, and film companies have become much more aware of this in recent years. I guess a lot changed after Lennon was shot, when we all realised that celebrities had become targets for obsessive nuts – it wasn't just politicians, popes and royalty that were in danger. As a result the way film sets operate has changed a bit. Now, for example, they always put the character's name rather than the actor's on the trailer, so that people who aren't involved in the project won't know quite what's going on. Similarly, production companies aren't allowed to print out a call sheet giving your personal details any more.

Derek Humphry had been a highly respected journalist on *The Sunday Times*. When his wife became terminally ill with cancer, he'd assisted her death. She died in his arms. He was taken to court and prosecuted, and for a while it looked as if he might be sent to prison. In the end he was released with a reprimand, but the story, of course, made national and international headlines. As the interest grew he became more and more engaged in the issues surrounding euthanasia, and began writing books, pamphlets and other material about it. Eventually he remarried, went to live in the States and built up quite a following.

The weird thing about Derek Humphry in the TV piece is that his interest starts to become obsessive. It also covers allegations about the assisted death of another family member whose wife starts to freak and to realise that Humphry's more than a bit strange. Once Humphry's followers found out that this stuff was in the script they got agitated. It's a very difficult subject and it was a terribly disturbing film, about which I still get a lot of letters.

The network put it out on TV one Saturday teatime when *Doctor Who* or something like that was on the other side. Dr Death on one side and Dr Who on the other – that seems like a bizarre thing to do!

I was cast alongside Gwen Humble for *Goodbye My Love*, an actress who is married to Ian McShane. They'd lived above me in a penthouse in Chelsea Harbour, or 'Divorce Alley' as I used to call it. They were one of the few married couples I knew who lived there – everyone else was divorced: Tom Stoppard lived two doors down from me; Sheridan Morley lived upstairs and, to top it all, Jim Davidson moved in.

Chelsea Harbour was the most soulless place. An episode of *My Family* was actually based around my experience of living there: Zoë Wanamaker (Susan) and I go and spend the weekend in a posh flat, and I'm trying to convince her that when the kids are gone we'll sell the house in Chiswick and buy one of these apartments. We tried to capture how anonymous Chelsea Harbour felt, how quiet and empty it was. In the *My Family* episode there's nobody else in the building: we order a takeaway pizza and the delivery guy can't find us because we're the only inhabitants in the block.

That's what it was actually like living in Chelsea Harbour. It was such a weird place. I nearly got arrested there once after going late night shopping. I couldn't find my entry card and set all the alarms off when I got back, with security pouncing on me in the car park. It was that kind of place.

Being newly single at Chelsea Harbour, all my old mates started turning up to see me. They would ring the buzzer, the face would come up on the screen and I'd press the button to let them in. That would be the last I saw of them for a while. They'd be wandering around Chelsea Harbour for ages trying to find the flat. Some probably still are!

I used to think I was *so* flash because Michael Caine and other well-known people lived at Chelsea Harbour. Michael had a penthouse with his wife Shakira (so another happily married couple *did* live in Chelsea Harbour!), but also had an involvement in a very stylish restaurant there called The Canteen. Princess Di used go swimming in the private club, a fact which I can personally vouch for. On the day concerned, I was the only other person in the swimming pool at The Harbour Club, learning to snorkel in preparation for a big holiday I was going on. There I was, wearing this ghastly swimming mask as I came up out of the water and saw Princess Di about to dive in. "Oh! Hi!" I said, wheezing the words out through my snorkel like some kind of damp Darth Vader. It had happened to me again. The previous time we met I was togged up to look like a coatimundi. This time I was in snorkel and flippers! I'm sure she found me irresistible.

On weekends, everyone used to disappear to France or to their country estates and all the divorcees were left entertaining their children. It wasn't long before I'd had enough. Rosemarie Ford and I had allowed our affair to flourish and I realised that she was the person I wanted to spend my life with. I did not want her to have to move into Chelsea Harbour, so we decided to buy somewhere that would work as a home for my daughter as well as us. We found the house in *Country Life*. Syd was mad keen on ponies then (she still is!), and what she actually said that Saturday teatime was: "We've found a stable." I rang and just caught the estate agents, viewed the house on the Sunday and, by Monday night, the deal was done. I still live there.

Soon after we moved in, I agreed to do *Oliver!* at the Palladium. I became very friendly with the show's writer, Lionel Bart, and he used to come out to the house for Sunday lunch. We used to sit by the river, me and him. "I love it 'ere Bob," he'd say. "I love it 'ere. It's lovely… I don't like the country but it's only eight miles from Acton! I love it when you can hear the aeroplanes." That summed it all up for me. There was me thinking I was living some rural idyll like a country gent and in fact I was doing it because it was only eight miles from Acton. He'd got it in one.

He used to sit in a willow seat I'd placed by the river. I was going to put 'Lionel Bart sat here' on it but unfortunately the seat planted itself and has now become a huge tree. Not liking to be out in the sticks, Lionel used to freak out as soon as he was in the country and he'd get a bit wobbly. He was a real city man – I think he would have tarmac'd everything beyond the M25 if he could have done.

Spending time with Lionel made me realise what a great character he was. He was full of stories. He claimed he'd been a drug baron for the Rolling Stones and that the briefcase he'd used to deliver all the goodies around the West End had ended up in the Police Museum. He used to throw great, wild parties where he'd give out beautiful presents to everyone. It was very sad to see Lionel at the end of his life; this most flamboyant of human beings reduced almost to a shell by cancer. He was a genius who really didn't have any business skills at all, and it was tragic that his creativity hadn't proved as financially worthwhile for him as it should have done.

I think Cameron Mackintosh ensured that Lionel made some money from that final production of *Oliver!*, a show that Lionel had signed away the copyright on, many years ago. Apparently, he didn't even make much money from the film having sold the rights for a pittance. It is, without doubt, one of the greatest film versions of a musical, ever.

When I was doing *Oliver*! Lionel would come along to the theatre all the time. He was lonely and loved company, so I used to go to his house in Acton and have a cup of tea with him, or go to the barbers with him in Acton High Street. Everyone knew him as he was a really sociable bloke.

He loved my Fagin! I know he did. He just absolutely loved the cheekiness of it and its darkness. He was the one who let me do 'the nose'. Cameron, the producer, and Sam Mendes, the director, vetoed the prosthetic nose. They said, "No, we don't want that. It's a children's show." And I said, "Well, sorry, but if you don't have the nose, you don't have me." Lionel stuck up for me and said, "No, he's right. He's right." Eventually they went with it (you could say we won by a nose) and it worked out really well. I thought I had a real edge in that performance. I was fortunate to have a great Bill Sykes in that show – Steven Hartley, from the north but with a well-developed London accent and a very deep voice. He was frightening as Bill, helping to give the show the real menace that it needs to balance the sweetness and purity of the way Oliver is presented.

The problem with *Oliver!* is that you have an eight-week turn-around on the show, so you have to re-rehearse with a new batch of kids every two months. That said, some of the child actors in *Oliver!* were excellent. Some of them still write to me, the Artful Dodgers and the Olivers. Four of them came to see *The Entertainer* recently. All these burly blokes came into my dressing room. One really big guy said, "Alright Bob?" I went, "Hello?" He said, "I was your Artful Dodger." These days he runs a company in Clacton. I thought, 'God, was it that long ago? Am I still going?'

TWENTY

TENSIONS
ON STAGE

WITH THE Bleasdales under my belt I felt like I'd put the Hollywood nightmare behind me (not that it didn't still hurt). I was back in England and working with some of the best in the business once again. In particular I collaborated with the director Elijah Moshinsky, having first worked with him after doing *GBH* in the early 1990s. He was a mysterious character but I really liked him and we got on terribly well. Previously he'd spent most of his time directing opera, establishing a reputation for wonderful vision with some great productions. It was Elijah who introduced me to opera by taking me to the Royal Opera House to see Zeffirelli's *La Bohème*. "Wow, this is theatre," I announced, before Elijah cautioned me with, "Yes, but it's expensive theatre." "Can't we do that in the theatre in such a way that it looks expensive but isn't?" I asked. And so it began, a working relationship that spanned much of the 1990s.

The first thing we did was *Becket*. Visually, it was stunning – and I mean really stunning – from the very first entrance, where my Henry II was about to be lashed, all the way through to the end when I'm on the plain with Becket, as played by Derek Jacobi. It was a monster of a hit. I remember going to the Haymarket every night, being excited seeing the queues around the block for that production. The play just looked so good, and that was largely down to Elijah and his designer, Michael Yeargan, an American who had created designs for a lot of his operas.

Becket was followed by *Cyrano de Bergerac,* which looked even better. The stills I've got from that production are just breathtaking. The cast and crew collected the images together for me in a book, which even has the plume from my Cyrano hat in it. Of the photographs, the last image of Roxanne and Cyrano, with the leaves falling on stage and the moon rising in the background, is just beautiful.

John Gielgud didn't recognise me when he came backstage to see me on the Royal Gala night because I had the long, 'funny' Cyrano nose on. "Where's Robert?" He was looking straight at me as he asked the question. "John, it's me." "Oh my God!" he said. "I didn't recognise you with that nose on." I stated the obvious: "Well, I *am* playing Cyrano de Bergerac." God love him.

On another night, Peter O'Toole came into my dressing room after the show with his son Lorcan. He said to Lorcan: "That's it, that's how to do it, that's acting!" I'd just got my trousers off after the show and was half way through dealing with the wig and the nose, when the next thing I knew he had picked me up and was parading me around the dressing room. He was surprisingly strong. It got my spirits up, but put my back out. I slipped a disc and missed three shows. It was almost worth it to have a legend like Peter O'Toole saying such nice things about me and the show. He came to see *The Entertainer* more recently and I said, "Don't touch me!"

Cyrano de Bergerac was a big success and ran for ten months or so, playing to virtually full houses all the way through. *Becket* had run for a year with a ten-week tour before the nine months in the West End. That was the Moshinsky Midas touch at work.

Becket's critical acclaim and popularity with audiences made it a really exciting production to be in. For a straight play to command that kind of response – to get great reviews and to be sold out – was just unprecedented. People were begging for tickets.

Originally, the plan was to alternate the two roles – the King and Becket – between myself and Derek Jacobi, but then Derek and I chatted and he said, "No, I think the problem is that we'll get too attached to our roles." He didn't think we'd be able to swap between the two so easily.

Derek, more than any other actor I've worked with, is extremely poetic; a wonderfully complex person with a very powerful stage presence. I have a feeling that, at that point in my life, I was very full of myself. I suspect that playing the role of Henry II filled me with a kind of arrogance and, with the role of Becket that Derek had, there was an inevitable clash of personalities. I know I was being extremely macho during this production, which is what I thought the role called for, whilst Derek became more and more introspective as Becket and I began to sense a growing friction between us.

I think Derek struggled with my apparent flippancy, or rather the way in which I inhabited my role, and I do admit that once again I developed a rapport with the audience in certain scenes. Becket and Henry II are juxtaposed as characters; one is the rebellious, anarchic, free-loving, free-drinking King and Becket – although intellectually superior – has to behave as an inferior as he is 'owned' by the King. The play is about occupation and ownership.

Matters all came to a head during one performance of a scene where Henry was raping a local Saxon girl and luring Becket to join in. Of course, in the script, Becket can only watch, with the audience aware of his inner turmoil. In a totally unrehearsed manner, Derek slapped me across the face. I was furious and shocked. After all, how could he slap the King? It wasn't in the script. You don't slap kings without others shouting 'off with his head'! We stared at each other, realising that although we were in this magnificent production, our styles of acting were completely different; now the point had been made. We never discussed the incident again and carried on in the private world of our own performances.

I knew that I'd crossed the line at one curtain call when I jokingly said to Derek, "For God's sake, Bish (archbishop), smile!" which was met with a glare. In fairness to me, Jane Howell at Exeter had always taught us that curtain calls were to be taken as 'you'. You dropped the character and came on to say thank you. But Derek was from a different tradition where you took the curtain call in character; again our styles clashed.

Sometimes, this clash of styles can be very productive – as indeed it was for *Becket*, two great roles demanding great performances. The production was one of the highlights of my career but it illustrated that actors and egos form a dangerous, combustible material.

Incidentally, it was during the *Becket* run – of all things – that Michael Aspel ambushed me for *This is Your Life*. I was absolutely horrified when Michael came on stage behind me, ready to pounce with his big red book, while I was trying to give the performance of the year!

After *Becket* and *Cyrano de Bergerac*, I worked with Elijah again, this time on a TV film, *Genghis Cohn*. The film also featured Antony Sher and Diana Rigg and was another success. Tony Sher was playing Genghis Cohn and I was playing Otto Schatz, the German officer who had him shot in a prison camp. Genghis Cohn comes back as a ghost after the war, by which time Schatz has become chief of police in some Bavarian town. Cohn haunts and begins to 'jew-ify' the character. There are some very funny scenes where I'm offering Diana Rigg's character gefilte fish and chopped liver saying 'shalom' whilst dressed as a Hitler lookalike. What was slightly perverse about the finished film was that the sympathy was going towards my character. We hadn't expected that interpretation at all, but the audience reaction was brought home to us in a Q & A session at the London Film Festival, when an elderly Jewish woman from the back thanked us for helping her to forgive.

I do feel that the way I engage with an audience can sometimes cause a problem for other actors. Do they think that I deliberately set out to steal the show? Is it professional rivalry? Or merely a clash of approach and attitude?

Michael Coveney, a theatre critic, once interviewed me in a platform discussion at The Old Vic. He suggested that everything I'd done in my career, including *Me and My Girl* and *The Entertainer*, involved me playing both to the audience and to the actors on stage and that I am as 'aware' of entertaining the crowds as I am of playing the character. Perhaps it's this that can rub other actors up the wrong way.

When I was in *Godspell*, one of the original cast members from the David Essex days returned to the show, a guy who's a big star now. We were halfway through the show when I noticed that this actor had started to be very physical with me. Something wasn't quite right. We did the curtain call and as we came off he just punched me straight in the face, and I mean a full blow. I saw red and started hitting him back – it was a full-on fight! The other actors tried to intervene. I remember Mary Magdalene jumped on my back, pulling me off, and there was Jesus piling in.

As it was one of those 'hippy' shows, everyone shared a dressing room and make-up together, which, after the fight, was awkward to say the least. The actor in question didn't speak to me for two weeks – he just stared into his make-up mirror every night.

Tina, a friend in the show at the time, thought he was irritated by the amount of attention the audience was giving me and by what I was doing to get it. So perhaps Michael Coveney has a point. Maybe this actor thought I was 'playing' the audience and he resented it.

I don't deliberately try and upstage people, but I think I do engage with the audience. That's not necessarily a bad thing: when you are a member of the audience you want to be engaged, to be lured over the footlights and into the action. You have to bring the character alive for them, to the point where the audience feel like they're experiencing what you are. Maybe other actors think 'this guy is so engaged with the audience that I've 'lost' them for my character'. It may come down to a clash of styles. Some actors aren't necessarily 'emotion rich', yet feel they ought to be. Given my style, it's easier for me to engage with the other players *and* the audience – I try and take both with me. I like to think of myself as a team or ensemble player. I'm not on a solo bid for stardom. I'm saying, let's all go together on this journey on stage.

If you really take the audience with you they suspend their

disbelief, they forget that they're in a West End theatre or a TV studio on a rainy Thursday night. You're then less likely to lose them should things go slightly off plan. There have been a few occasions on *My Family* when Zoë Wanamaker has said to me, "How do you do that? I don't know how you manage to take the audience with you. If we go wrong, I just freak, but you go wrong and then keep the audience going. Nothing seems to worry you or them and you make everyone feel comfortable... you just seem so confident to go out of character, off script, and then come back in."

It again comes down to being part actor, part performer. While my head yearns to be taken seriously, my heart has always had a soft spot for the pure entertainment side of what I do. That's probably why the sitcom turned out to be such a good medium for me.

Clearly you have to strike a balance between playing the character and playing the audience and, if push comes to shove, you've got to choose that authenticity over relating to the audience. I was always in danger of not doing that when I played Archie Rice in *The Entertainer*. Because of the nature of the role, it was always tempting to take the easy option and play to the audience. But the director's notes were always in my head: "He doesn't like the audience; he's a bad entertainer." So I wouldn't allow myself to compromise the character.

Anyway, back to Elijah and *Genghis Cohn*. During filming I began to realise that Elijah wasn't very well. Something was wrong. When I agreed much later on to do *Richard III* at the RSC, I helped to get him appointed as director, saying that I must have Elijah for the production. They were thinking of someone else, but I wanted Elijah because I knew he could make it superb. But then he began disappearing during rehearsals. The cast became increasingly restless, suspicious about what was going on.

He'd always 'disappeared' occasionally, even during *Becket* and *Cyrano de Bergerac.* He'd slope off to do some opera in Chicago at the most inopportune moment. We struggled manfully through *Richard III,* but it was a very unhappy rehearsal period.

I found I was constantly apologising for his absence and ended up taking the rehearsals myself on many days. I began to realise that the production wouldn't measure up to what I'd envisaged before we started out. In the event it did better than I thought it was going to – in fact, some of the reviews were quite remarkable, considering. On the opening night at the RSC, the stage manager told me that Elijah had sent a message saying he wouldn't be there because he'd had to go to Chicago to do an opera. "What?" I moaned. "On the first night!" I had a parade of angry actors coming up to me: "This is your f***ing friend. You're going to have to do this. Where is he?"

Despite the problems, *Richard III* came at just the right time for me. I was feeling more secure. I'd done a stint of the commercial West End stuff with *Oliver!* and now, with the house in Buckinghamshire working out, Syd settled in Ibstock at her new school and a new and comfortable friendship forged with Diana, I had the chance to do something for me as it were. We rehearsed the production in the RSC's south London rehearsal rooms for four or five weeks (with or without Elijah), and then I went to live up in Stratford-upon-Avon. I hated the place. I thought it was like living in Disneyland, but with Oberon, Macbeth and co holding the fort while Mickey and friends were taking a fag break.

The play opened to what I suppose we would call mixed reviews. Benedict Nightingale hailed me as the new Olivier in *The Times*, while another reviewer, Michael Billington, compared me to Ken Dodd. I sent Michael a jokey Christmas card based on his comparison. When a photographer came in to take some publicity shots for the tour of *Richard III*, after we opened at Stratford, I turned myself into a kind of Richard Dodd III character: dressed as the King with his hump, but carrying a tickling stick instead of a sceptre. I stuck the photo on a card, wrote 'Happy Christmas, from Ken Lindsay' inside and sent it off. I never heard back.

My first night at the RSC and everything that could go wrong did go wrong: the director was AWOL, I was feeling ill and then, to top it all, we had an electrical failure and couldn't start the show. The opening night in London at the Savoy Theatre was similarly blighted when the scenery chains refused to come down, probably *the* most dramatic fault of the lot. I thought that kind of stuff was only supposed to happen when you did *Macbeth*!

On the morning after the Stratford opening, I woke to calls from the press – they were all there on a 'junket' and wanted to get an interview before heading back to London. The RSC rang me up and said, "We're recording *Front Row* live for Radio Four in our studio underneath the stage. Can you be here at half past ten?" Overnight, my illness seemed to have turned into raging flu, and I was still in shock that my director had gone to Chicago to direct an opera and that I was therefore left to front the whole production. Not the ideal preparation for taking to the airwaves.

"Congratulations. I've just read the Benedict Nightingale review," said the interviewer. "Thank you very much," I replied.

"Although," she continued, "some of them have been less than kind, haven't they?" "Honestly," I stressed, "I haven't read them." But she came back with: "You *must* have done." I repeated: "I haven't read them." I was in the basement of the RSC, in a bad mood, with flu, thinking, 'Who wants to be in this f***ing profession anyway?' And then she made the mistake of asking: "What do you think of Stratford?" I really went to town. I told her that living in Stratford was like living in a theme park.

Shortly after the interview, my mobile rang and it was my dad greeting me with: "Why can't you shut your bloody mouth?" "What?" I said, taken aback. "Did you have to say all that," he continued. "Go and hide. You always have to do it, don't you?"

The interview caused uproar. You wouldn't believe the letters I got or the anger I managed to generate with those remarks. I was getting hate mail. I couldn't even go out for a meal after the show; restaurants were refusing to serve me. The RSC were getting sacks of mail too, all of it complaining. They told me I had to make an apology to the good burghers of Stratford.

Something had to be done, so we set up a *Richard III* Q & A at the theatre, which was packed with the aforementioned good burghers of Stratford. I realised that I had to say something to try and make amends, so I explained what I had been going through, how I had felt and that sometimes I reacted impulsively and emotionally and so on. I just about got out of it I think, or at least I did with the people who were there in the audience that night.

They were saying to me things like, "What on earth do you mean, a theme park?" I said, "Well, it's as if there's a Romeo and Juliet café and a Falstaff bowling alley. You can buy Shakespeare soap-on-a-rope. Everything in this town is about

Shakespeare." I tried to explain that, as an actor at the RSC, when you step out on stage and the auditorium is full of tourists it can feel rather like you're performing a special stage show in a theme park. So, I guess I went for honesty. They weren't pleased but I managed to avoid a stint in the town stocks.

We did, however, take *Richard III* to the Savoy Theatre in the West End and it played to full houses. One particular night, I came on to begin the famous soliloquy (the one parodied beautifully by a camping store as 'Now is the winter of our discount tents'!). As I started, I became aware of someone muttering. Slowly the mumbling became more audible and I realised that someone was repeating my lines. I looked down and, to my horror, there on the front row, feet resting on the stage, drinking from a can of lager, was the stereotypical heckler. I stopped. He stopped. I started. He started. The audience had now become aware of the feud. Eventually I leaned down and, in a stage whisper, said, "If you know the lines, then get up here and say them," to which he replied, "I'm not as good an actor as you Mr Lindsay." "Well, you're making a good job of it," I said, "but now you can shut up or get out." And, to my amazement, he stood up and walked out. However, he did insist on waiting outside the stage door every night as he thought we had become buddies. I know I said earlier that I like to engage with the audience, but this was stretching it!

In all, I was in *Richard III* for a year, after three years in *Me and My Girl*, a year in *Becket*, a year in *Cyrano de Bergerac* and a year in *Oliver!* These are big chunks of my life! After the long run playing Fagin in *Oliver!* at the Palladium, I'd made up my mind, having gone through two broken long-term relationships and now having a daughter, that I needed some normality in my life. I didn't feel like I could have a normal, sensible relationship while I was doing these long back-to-back runs on stage, and, having recently settled down with Rosemarie Ford, I didn't want to jeopardise this relationship. I was looking for a regular job.

Around the same time, I met the writer and producer Fred Barron. "Why don't you do a sitcom again? They're so life-friendly!" he said, after I told him about going off to New York, about doing all these long runs and about how I now needed a change. "I'll write you one," he said. "We'll go to the BBC and get it done, the pair of us." Off we went to see the Head of Light Entertainment, Geoffrey Perkins. After he heard the outline, he asked, "What are you going to call it?" "*My Family*," I said, off the top of my head. Fred went, "What?" I said, "I want to call it *My Family*." Fred wanted to call it *Trouble with Ben* or something like that – something that referred to my on-screen character.

I knew it was going to be a hit from the off. I also knew it would allow me to settle down and get a normal life. I keep sending little 'thank you' notes to Fred for giving that to me.

We needed a clever actress to play my wife in the show, an actress who could be funny and was also a bit quirky. I was in The Ivy one evening after going to see a show in the West End with my friend Ron Cook, when the actor Gawn Grainger walked in with his wife, Zoë Wanamaker. I clicked my fingers in an 'I've got it' moment and said to Ron, "Zoë... f***ing brilliant." I went over to Zoë and said, "You don't fancy playing my wife in a TV comedy series, do you?" The next thing we knew she was doing it.

It had been a long time since I'd done a sitcom. I didn't do a sitcom at all for the whole of the 1980s, a fact that has only dawned on me whilst writing this book. I'd done *Get Some In*, *Citizen Smith*, *Seconds Out* and *Nightingales* in the 1970s, but nothing in the 1980s.

My first introduction to the world of sitcom was a small part in *Doctor in the House*, playing an intern with about five lines. One gag involved bringing ten donkeys out onto the set, surprising the studio audience and hopefully generating a big laugh. I was only twenty or twenty-one at the time, and I proudly thought here I am on TV, recording at London Weekend Studios. Humphrey Barclay was producing the show and he used to do the studio audience warm-up as well. I was standing at the back with Richard O' Sullivan, star of the show, thinking, 'This is going to be great. The audience have no idea that ten donkeys are about to appear.'

But as part of his warm-up routine, Humphrey Barclay then announced: "And tonight, we are going to welcome to the studio our youngest actor on the set, a debutant here, Robert Lindsay and, for their first time on TV... ten donkeys!" Richard and I together went, "Oh, f***ing hell." Of course, when it came to doing the actual gag later on, the element of surprise had totally gone so there was nothing from the audience... just complete silence. You could have heard a donkey fart.

TWENTY-ONE

GETTING POLITICAL

IT'S STRANGE how the things that I've enjoyed doing least in my career seem to have been the most successful, while the stuff that I've really liked doing hasn't done so well, perhaps with the exception of *Me and My Girl* and *GBH* – both of which I absolutely loved working on and which were very well received. There's a definite pattern there.

Friends and Crocodiles and *Gideon's Daughter* both make it onto the 'not very enjoyable but quite successful' list. Both were Stephen Poliakoff films made for TV in 2005. Critically they had a mixed response, but they looked wonderful and had plenty of style. I played the same character in both, a social climber called Sneath.

Stephen is a wonderful writer and a great man. As a director, he can be very strict and, although I couldn't really understand the progression of my character between the two films, Stephen wouldn't let me do particular things that I thought might help. I had a certain someone in mind to model the character on, but Stephen said no. He vetoed everything I suggested. Usually, I get at least some of my own way and, having a vivid imagination, I have a few good initial ideas as I think about what I want to do. I'm not saying that I'm always right though, just that I don't think that I am always wrong! Anyway, the whole thing left me with a rather empty feeling.

In contrast, I really enjoyed both the Tony Blair roles that I played in 2005 and 2006. David Aukin was responsible for getting me to do both projects. I've got a lot of history with David, from an early play at Hampstead Theatre through *Me and My Girl* and on to the Bleasdales when he was Head of Films at Channel Four. After that, he went on to work with Miramax and Harvey Weinstein, and is currently Head of Drama at Mentorn Media. He's been a big influence on my career and is a guy I really trust and admire, so much so that he recently persuaded me to play Aristotle Onassis on stage – but that really *is* another book!

David asked me to do *A Very Social Secretary* by Alistair Beaton, the first Blair TV film, a feature-length satire based around the David Blunkett affair that broke in 2004 after it was revealed that the Home Secretary was in a relationship with Kimberly Quinn, a married woman. It helps that I trust David Aukin's judgement completely, which is crucial if you are going to get involved in politically sensitive stuff.

The second Blair piece was *The Trial of Tony Blair*, also by Beaton, another satire but this time fictitious. Set shortly after Blair has reluctantly handed the top job over to Gordon Brown, the drama ends with Blair being hauled off to a tribunal in The Hague, accused of waging illegal war on Iraq.

Even though I was Blair in both, they were two very different films for me to play. The first was the most straightforward in many ways. Really I was doing a loose impression of Tony Blair

– something I thought I could do well – in what was, for my part, a series of sketches. The impressionist Rory Bremner actually gave me some help in preparing for the role. "Never let him out of your mind. Just think of him constantly," he said, adding that he thought that I was a good enough actor to get away with it anyway.

The second film required a completely different approach. I had the main part all the way through and knew that I would have difficulty sustaining it as a continuous accurate impersonation. The problem was that when I got it right and the impression was spot on, the crew would always laugh. That's when I realised what mimicry is all about – that it makes you laugh because you are making a comment about the person, but not actually trying to make the audience believe that you are that real person with their real problems.

Simon Cellan Jones, the director, and I discussed it. "Just drop it," he said. "Don't think about it. Don't think about doing an impersonation, just play what's in the script, which is a man in turmoil."

I tried to construct and convey an 'interpretation' of Tony Blair rather than using outright, accurate mimicry. It can get boring watching someone simply impersonating a figure over a long period of time, because you don't believe that they are the character. So, I developed an interpretation of Tony Blair that was more impressionistic than an impression (if that makes sense!). I only used elements of the real Blair to create the desired effect. Of course, I had to get the physical resemblance right – the mannerisms, facial expressions and body movements – but he had to be a believable human portrait too. TB or not TB, again!

Neither film was easy to do. They were made quickly and on

a small budget. They were hit-and-run productions, where it's 'bang, bang, bang', probably doing about ten scenes a day and having to motor through it in a small amount of time. It was really hard graft – you had to know the part without any time for busking around.

At the time I was asked if it was difficult, not only having to learn the lines and moves but also to impersonate someone. In reality, the impersonation distracted me less and less as the filming progressed, although I had the odd panic about it and kept feeling like I had to use elements of it to remind the viewers it was him. I don't think I'll win any awards for mimicry, but I do think I achieved a believable character that people would become interested in and, ironically, feel quite sorry for.

The Trial of Tony Blair was a powerful piece on a controversial subject. The emotive content was one of the reasons I got involved. It bugged me that Tony Blair, as a religious man, a family man, could send all those people to war. Having kids of my own, I kept thinking, 'How do you live with that?' He's never shown any kind of remorse, in public at least, no doubt because he thought that it *was* the right thing to do at the time.

I don't believe people when they say they have no regrets because people are full of regrets and doubts. There have always got to be doubts, but Tony Blair has never shown any. You might say that you can't afford to show doubt if you're running the country, but I guess I wasn't interested in the man running the country, I was more interested in the human being who was in his kitchen at night watching the news, treading amongst his children's toys.

We invented the young Iraqi boy in the TV clips to give the script what we thought it needed: a darker aspect. Blair's nightmares, the flashbacks of seeing terrorists and then discovering the boy in a blown-out kitchen, worked remarkably well, I think, because they were quite shocking scenes.

In one minor physical way, the films differed – I wore coloured contact lenses in the first but not the second. I had real trouble with them in *A Very Social Secretary*, and taking them out at the end of a day's filming was a nightmare. I would panic when I couldn't get them out straight away. I did wear them for one scene at the beginning of the second film, in the very extreme close-up of the TV interview. The problem with TV is that things like that don't show. On a 35mm movie they would have been seen, but anything less, on 16mm and below, it just doesn't show up, so it's hardly worth the pain. The lenses were left out. However I did have the teeth! Tony Blair has a gap in his front teeth, so I had the same look. He'll probably be able to afford to have it fixed now from the fees he's earning on those foreign trips saving the world. Tony Blair as a Middle East envoy. What an irony. I sometimes wonder if he watched either of the films, particularly the second one.

For all that, I'm still Labour. Where else would I go? I watched the town I grew up in disintegrate under the Tories. That's why I have such an affinity with Alan Bleasdale. He saw something very similar happen in Liverpool, with all the social consequences of industrial decline, although in his case he's never left his home town. He is very proud of his roots and won't leave, but I left Ilkeston and now I live in leafy Buckinghamshire on the outskirts of London, or as Lionel Bart would have it, 'eight miles from Acton'.

My life has gone through a big change since I left Ilkeston, so I always feel slightly unsteady climbing up onto the soapbox.

I know people could shoot me down and say, "Yeah, well, you're a rich television star now, so what have you got to spout on about?" But I know where I come from and I now know who I am. I go back home regularly, and can walk about the town freely as people tend to leave me alone. I see people up there, struggling to make ends meet, always counting the pennies because they have to. I don't deny that I wanted to escape that, but I am still very aware of it.

I do feel very left-of-centre politically and I've always supported the people, the working man, or what used to be called the working man. I think my values are pre-New Labour, but the irony is that I live a life that would be considered to be one of luxury by the working man – I'm more extravagant than I should be. Just to complicate matters, I am a bit of a recluse because I don't like being recognised, so I hardly give the impression of being a 'man of the people'. But I'm always reminded of my roots and they always drag me back. They come through in my approach to life – it sometimes seems that I've done everything that people have told me not to, something, I think, which stems from that rather 'dark', working-class East Midlands persona.

Diana Weston always used to say that I had a terrible chip on my shoulder. "You'll never learn anything unless you lose that chip," she would say. She was probably right. Diana is, I suppose, upper middle class, but she adored my parents and loved the sense of having a close family – something she'd never had. She loved the fact that my parents had been married for many years and had always lived in the same two-up, two-down. She understood where I came from, but she also said: "If you dismiss my lot as chinless 'upper-class twits' you'll never learn anything.

Because they're not – they're just as insecure as your lot."

She actually taught me a great deal about class, in fact, Diana taught me about friendship. Even meeting her slightly barmy stepfather had its educational value. He smashed a table on one occasion because I was talking about two working-class boys in Newcastle who'd committed suicide. We were having Sunday lunch with them down in Bath and he was a bit drunk. I got very upset about these two boys, because they'd left a note saying there was no future for them. As I talked I could see smoke coming out of his ears. Perhaps he got the wrong end of the stick, but he suddenly stood up and said, "There's no such thing as the working class. It's all in the mind." Whereupon he thumped his hand down and smashed the table. It collapsed and the dinner went everywhere – all over Diana's mum, also tiddly, who merely said, "Are we going to play Cluedo now?"

Diana ran off in tears and I went up to get my bags. "I can't stay in this place with that awful man," I said. She calmed me down and we wrote this note:

'When talking of class
We can open our arse
And prove that our thoughts are unstable.
We can all shout and scream
The solution's a dream
But f*** it!
We don't have to smash the table.'

I don't think my working-class indignation has ever served me particularly well. Indeed, looking back now, I can see that on occasion all it did was to limit my experiences. When I was in *Becket*, my co-star Derek Jacobi invited me to join him and Margaret Thatcher for dinner one evening. I declined. She ended up in my dressing room demanding to know why I wasn't going out with them. She left Dennis upstairs with Derek and came down to see me: "I gather from Derek you aren't joining us at The Savoy," she said, to which I bravely ventured: "No, ma'am. Actually I don't agree with your politics." In response, she quipped: "Well that doesn't affect your appetite does it?" All I could reply was, "Yes, it does affect it, I'm afraid!"

She kind of ambushed me. I was on my own, still wearing my crown from the performance, starting to get undressed. She was standing there in shimmering black, proclaiming that, "The thing about Henry is that he was a very confused man. And Becket was a really good person with a genuine sense of goodness that Henry couldn't understand."

I got slightly paranoid. She's trying to tell me that I'm really crap, I thought. She's saying that both Henry and I were uneducated and that she was happy to leave me behind and to go out with Becket. I don't see it like that now. All I think is what a waste of an opportunity – I could have had dinner with Mrs Thatcher. Even though I thought I was taking a principled stand because of my political views, now it seems a bit daft when I could have learned more about her. Sometimes, principles can get in the way.

Perhaps I've made the same mistakes that John Osborne did. He had his working-class chip too, and he was desperate to be taken seriously, legitimately. What does he do? He becomes rich and famous, buys himself a country estate, starts to wear brogues, to speak terribly 'posh' and becomes everything he was previously fighting against. Maybe I've rejected certain people unnecessarily. Class is absolutely pointless if you let it prevent you learning from people who are different from yourself.

I don't think the social divide in Britain today is based on class as much as it was. It's more about the American thing of money. There are those who have and there are those who have not, and that is a whole lot worse than the old divide. The old structure could be coped with; the structure that was there when *The Entertainer* was written and when I grew up in the Fifties. If you were lucky, you could go up the ladder. Now, it's as if you push your way up using violence and aggression. I think it generates real hatred, born perhaps of envy. I can see it sometimes when people approach me. If I say, "Oh I'm very, very sorry, I've got to rush," I can see them thinking, 'Who do you think you are?'

The preoccupation with money and possessions comes from the States. It's the bling, rap and celebrity thing that children aspire to, and which I loathe. There have always been celebrities, but it becomes dangerous when celebrity and fame are seen as being more important than talent, skill and technique.

TWENTY-TWO

PLAYING DETECTIVE

IT'S IRONIC that some years ago I was offered the role of Cracker; indeed I worked with Gub Neal, the producer, and the writer Jimmy McGovern on the role, but at the last moment I got cold feet and realised that I didn't want to be in a detective series, albeit one with a distinctive take. Ouch, you may say, but there's a bigger ouch to come. When I finally decided to play a detective, it was in the TV series, *Jericho*, which was to be a huge disappointment, particularly as I had such high hopes for it. It was one of those – a piece that I really enjoyed doing but which wasn't a big success. I played Michael Jericho, a distinguished Scotland Yard DI from the 1950s. The series had a lot of hype and was well trailed and advertised before it was aired, but it just seemed to get lost.

Perhaps it was too long, although people love *Midsomer Murders*, which uses the same slot on a Sunday night. It's a similar story with *Poirot*, although the leads in both of these shows are more viewer-friendly than Jericho was.

It had a good cast, was atmospheric and easy on the eye.

They used Cinematic Graphics (computer generated imagery, or CGI) to create an authentic Fifties feel for the backdrops of Piccadilly Circus and Soho. The CGI stuff only cost thirty thousand pounds whereas on a film it would have cost five or six million. Even so, I still think some of *Jericho* is absolutely stunning to watch.

I chose to do *Jericho* because of the 1950s setting, a very interesting period to explore. I really wanted to create a Humphrey Bogart-type character – a loner with the mac, the trilby, the cigarette, the whole thing, but I don't think I pulled it off. I should have given him a harder edge. I had a slight divergence of views with the writer Stewart Harcourt – he wanted a heroic figure, whereas I wanted a dark loner. I think the character should, perhaps, have been fleshed out more.

We realised we couldn't simply recreate the TV coppers of the 1950s; the script needed more realism. Using the uncomplicated scenarios of old, with the police on one side saying 'you're nicked' and the villains on the other admitting 'it's a fair cop', would have produced parody. We had to give *Jericho* more of an edge for a modern audience. And so the series has this menacing *noir* feel, with a lead character who is honest but dark, who carries around an air of tragedy.

Here was a Jewish East Ender, from Bethnal Green, whose father was gunned down in front of him when he was just a boy, an event which haunted him in the programme through a series of flashbacks. The idea for that came from an incident in my brother's life. He'd witnessed a shooting when he was a teenager and the image of it stayed with him for years – he had trouble sleeping for a long time. Stewart and I discussed the development of these ideas for *Jericho*. We also decided to introduce a prostitute as a love interest. People found that a bit difficult to take (even though prostitutes were common in Fifties Soho), especially when, in one scene, she was selling her wares. It doesn't matter how beautiful she is, it isn't really Sunday-night material.

Part of the issue with *Jericho* was that the scripts weren't quite ready when filming started, and so in some instances they felt rushed. One script was even vetoed at the last minute whilst we were filming, prompting a swift rewrite from Stewart. The first show, directed by Nick Renton, had three different plots and ended up being very convoluted. I think the audience lost track of it and then, of course, we lost viewers on the next three episodes.

The first outing did the damage. We got five and a half million viewers, not bad for a Sunday night, although you can get anything up to eight or nine million, which is what *Midsomer Murders* gets. I think people want easier viewing on a Sunday night. They've got work tomorrow, they just want to sit back, have a nice glass of wine, avoid thinking about the coming week and relax into something on the telly. *Jericho* didn't quite find that niche.

What *Jericho* did do though, from a personal point of view, was to help in the process of writing this book because it prodded me into 'playing detective', investigating the 1950s of my youth. I wrote various articles about the series for the press and it made me realise how many memories and anecdotes I had to draw on. It also made me appreciate how immeasurably life has changed since then.

I accept that society develops, that change is inevitable, but the fall in basic values over the last half century really worries me. Morality has declined, while material wealth has supposedly increased. Having been through the hell of the Second World

War, people in the 1950s were overprotective. That's why the important images of the time all centred on the safety of the family, usually gathered around the table listening to the radio. Back then everything was 'cosier'.

There were storybook heroes to aspire to, characters who embodied courage and loyalty. They were strong men like Stanley Matthews and Edmund Hilary – men who behaved with honour and dignity whatever the circumstances. From Roy of the Rovers to PC George Dixon or Field Marshal Montgomery, these were the figures that led by example, stirring our spirits in childhood books or on that new wonder of the modern age, the television. Somewhere along the line, however, the inspiring paragons of popular culture changed – somehow PC Dixon morphed into Cracker.

Today we only seem to worship wealth and celebrity, and we're jealous of the people who achieve it. Back then we respected talent and ability, and saw those heroes as part of the community, not as something distant. They may have been above the people but they were also *of* the people. They'd achieved their success on genuine merit – how many celebrities can you say that about today? Nowadays too many seem to believe their own hype; they forget that really they're no different from the rest of us.

I remember hearing a story about Maurice Norman, an ex-Spurs and England footballer. He used to catch the bus to the games at White Hart Lane and would sit there chatting away to people on the journey. "You're not going to make it to the match in time," they would say. He would just shrug and say, "Of course I will." And then he'd light a fag. Can you imagine that happening today? Can you picture David Beckham standing at the bus stop, boot bag in hand? I once worked on a film project with another footballer, the great Tommy Lawton, and he told me similar stories about other England players of old, such as how the goalkeeper Frank Swift would pick up his cap from between the goalposts, take out his Woodbines and light up at half time. Real, down-to-earth heroes.

'Community' really meant something back then. I can remember being on the terraces with my dad at the Baseball Ground, aged ten, a small figure amid forty thousand others watching a cup match between Derby County and Manchester United. Before I knew what was going on, I was lifted above the reassuring fug of Woodbines and Kimberley Ale, carried aloft from hand to hand over spectators' heads and deposited pitch-side, only yards from the action. Amongst all those strangers, I'd never felt safer.

Doors were never locked and neighbours would wander in unannounced, guaranteed a friendly welcome. Out in the street we had parties, untroubled by the almost non-existent traffic. We spent summers by the canal, fishing and playing, and looked forward to the Sunday traditions of overcooked Brussels sprouts and brass bands in the park. They were my 1950s.

Setting the rose-tinted specs down for a moment, there was, of course, another 1950s. The war had left Britain badly scarred, physically and mentally; diseases like smallpox, tuberculosis and polio were still a danger, and some people lived in wretched slums while others worked in awful conditions in the mines just a mile or two from where I played. Then, as now, there were murderers and rapists (it's hard to get nostalgic about the Krays, Jack McVitie and John Christie). Not every copper was like PC Dixon, and corruption in the force was a problem. People had affairs, and children were born out of wedlock, but it was all swept under the carpet. No one talked about it. For the men returning from the front, theirs was a private trauma best left unmentioned.

For all that, I stand by my assertion that values have changed for the worse since the Fifties. It seems particularly tragic when you place it all in the context of those men who didn't return from the war. What would they make of what we've become? I've imagined a scene where two soldiers are fighting on the front line in North Africa or Europe in 1945 and one of them gets a flash of the future. It's so grim that he turns to his mate and says, "Why are we putting ourselves through this? All these sacrifices and for what – I've seen the future and it doesn't look good."

My Uncle Cyril died at that stage of the war rescuing a mate. Not so long ago we visited his grave just outside Florence on the banks of the beautiful River Arno. 'Sergeant George Cyril Stevenson' it reads. The Italian driver who took Rosie and I to see it was very distressed – he said he was sorry that we had to visit family buried in his country and not in our own.

Shortly before he was killed, my uncle had received a letter from his wife telling him of an affair. I am sure he thought, 'What's the point?' So much so that despite being held down by sniper fire, he went to rescue an injured mate who was calling out, "Cyril, Cyril, help me! Please." The officer-in-charge told everyone to stay where they were until the sniper had been dealt with, but Cyril ran over the line to go and get his mate. He picked him up and was pulling him back when he trod on a mine.

The sense of affinity that I have with the 1950s helped guide me toward another recent project, *The Entertainer*. It was written by a very Angry Young Man, John Osborne, back in 1957, but it has so many aspects and issues that still resonate today. He had a lot to say about the society he was living in, and did so with excellent observation. I'm not sure that Osborne was as intellectual in the formal, educated sense as, say, writer and director David Hare, but then again what is an intellectual? To me it's someone who is capable of changing the way we think, and Osborne certainly did that.

He used metaphor to comment on the decline of the British Empire, which he paralleled with the Empire theatres and the decline of Variety. Really he was writing about the decline of family life brought about by drink. That was going on then in the Fifties, as it is now, and if you were a man like John Osborne, a bohemian left-wing writer, you would discuss it in your work.

I was sheltered from all that as a child. My parents protected me from it, something that was easier to do back then because society's ills weren't plastered across newspapers and televisions in quite the same way that they are now. Children nowadays are much more aware of what is happening in the world. Everything is openly dealt with – murder, death, disease – all in graphic detail. We've lost our innocence. It 'went' somewhere and I suspect it was sometime in the Sixties, ostensibly an age of innocence, of flower-power, hippies and smoking cannabis, but also an age when people started exposing lies and telling the truth. Unfortunately the truth hurts, and now it affects all our lives. Perhaps ignorance really is bliss.

My route to *The Entertainer* was rather convoluted. It had been in the back of my mind since Laurence Olivier had suggested I should play Archie Rice one day when I was old enough, and I got the chance to perform a section of the show during a Royal Court event celebrating the play's fiftieth anniversary. That involved me giving a rehearsed reading for the aforementioned David Hare. David was terrific to work with. He'd known

John Osborne very well and, like John, his work offers savage commentary on the society he's living in. You have to admire people like that; they stand up to be counted. People like Hare and Osborne and Bleasdale, they're all writers who make a statement about the world in which they live.

Anyway, the rehearsed reading went well and received some very good reviews, prompting me to think about a full production. The Archie Rice part was one that I really wanted to play. I saw David Hare again in New York – I was there to see about playing a role in *Spamalot* – and I asked him, "Can't we do *The Entertainer* together in the West End?" He told me that Kevin Spacey owned the rights and suggested I write to him, which I duly did. Within a week, I got a phone call and the plot was hatched: we'd do *The Entertainer* at The Old Vic. David Hare was busy elsewhere, but Kevin had the idea of approaching Sean Holmes, a young director. He turned out to be fantastic – a real find. He allowed me to sit in the inventor's seat, letting me throw in ideas here and there but always keeping control of the bigger picture: he operates a bit like he's flying a kite, occasionally giving a little tug or not, as needs be, when things need to be pulled in or let out.

I enjoyed playing Archie Rice but there were a few issues with the audience. The rehearsed reading at the Royal Court had been given to a hundred or so intellectuals, journalists, theatre producers, directors and theatre trust members. The audience at The Old Vic was completely different. On some nights they loved it, on others they seemed rather nonplussed. I asked Pam Ferris, also in the play with me, what she thought the reason was. How could we get a euphoric reception one night, with cheering and a standing ovation, and then follow it the next night with silence?

In the last week of the run she came up with an answer. "We're established TV names, both of us, so on some nights we're bringing in audiences who have no preconceived idea of the play they're seeing," she said. "They are simply coming to see Pam Ferris from *The Darling Buds of May* and Robert Lindsay from *My Family*. They are our TV audience and they're asking, 'What the hell's this?'"

The penny dropped. At the performances when we had our TV 'following' in, the audience didn't really get the show, or if they did, they didn't know what to do with it. They didn't know how to take the play. The 'following' has expectations of you. They should be thinking 'that's Archie Rice up there on stage' but instead they were saying to themselves 'that's Robert Lindsay. That's the guy out of *My Family*'. Because the publicity for the show was so extensive – it was on buses, the Tube and in the papers – a lot of people thought I was *the* entertainer, rather than in *The Entertainer*.

We were getting the coach parties who usually go to see *Spamalot*, *The Sound of Music*, *The Producers*, *Me and My Girl* and so on. But *The Entertainer* isn't that kind of show. Archie doesn't like the audience within the play – he's crude and abusive to the imaginary 'them'. During those bits of the play you could feel the shock among the real audience. They couldn't believe that I, Robert Lindsay, was saying, in effect, "You bunch of shits – what are you doing here?" I had a real problem with it. So did they.

My cleaner came to see it with her family and I still don't know what she made of it. All she could manage to say to me on the Monday morning after the show was, "Saw you Saturday. You must be very tired." I don't think it was quite the fun night out she had been expecting.

That's the problem with carrying TV popularity over into the theatre. It's the problem with having two sides: a 'legit' theatre side and a light entertainment side. Leonard Rossiter had a similar problem. He was a wonderful actor, a really serious actor who was terrific in plays like *The Resistible Rise of Arturo Ui*, but by the time he was in *Rising Damp* the audience only really knew him as Rigsby. He found it difficult to shake off that preconception for his theatre stuff. It doesn't help that there's a real snobbery within the business itself that makes that crossover even harder, even if it doesn't prevent it happening altogether.

I've come to that stage in my career, the stage where it's getting harder and harder to take the audience with me into another world. I'm too familiar to them. The theatre is hard work and I've made it harder for myself by being well known; I'm recognised too easily as Robert Lindsay. It isn't that people aren't nice, they are: they smile and are friendly, but I have to confess I'm not comfortable with celebrity, not with my own or with its wider culture.

Perhaps I'm guilty of making a rod for my own back. Why do I feel like I have to constantly prove myself as a 'serious' actor, even at this age? Who am I trying to convince anyway? I've done the Ibsen, the Shakespeare, Osborne, Hare and Bleasdale; what do I have to prove? Perhaps it goes all the way back to failing the eleven-plus, to still feeling, even after forty-odd years, that I've got to 'get the right grades'.

I know I shouldn't moan. I've been lucky. My old PA used to tell me how unusual it was for an actor to be offered such diverse roles: "Just look at this: here's a musical, here's a Shakespeare. You've been offered this Chekhov. There's another sitcom here and, oh, you've got these voice-overs." But this diversity, the swings from comedy to tragedy, from Shakespeare to sitcom, have left me with a feeling that I am, perhaps, a 'Jack of all trades'. I've spent most of my life, or certainly the last forty years of it, being other people, wanting to be other people, watching other people, behaving like them. I'm not a method actor by any means, but I approach things with a great degree of honesty. I always feel that I have to inhabit the character to a certain extent to make it believable to an audience. I have to convince myself that I *am* that person. All of which makes it difficult to keep a hold of one *me*.

The most positive thing I can take from my career is that, by and large, people seem to like me. I think that's why Alan Bleasdale and David Aukin and others have used me to play dark characters, not simply because they see a certain melancholy in me, but because they also see a side that people can like and relate to. Even Ben Harper in *My Family*. He's horrible; he doesn't like his children, he moans at everything, but the audience love him. He's a malicious human being, but all the letters I get from kids say things like: "Oh I wish you were my dad." One letter said, "I'd love to be in your family, it's looks such fun." I've played some nasty buggers – Richard III included – but I always feel that, however villainous, they're not devoid of compassion; they have that ability to stir sympathy. Often they are just loveable rogues, aren't they?

Maybe that's me, a 'loveable rogue', although at my age the expression seems to belong to a much younger man.

I suppose I've played many parts. In life, I suspect I've been guilty of playing out roles when I should have been dealing with reality. But now my children need me to be their rock, their friend and their father (along with their chauffeur and their magical wizard!) and these roles I've written myself as I've gone along and they are very real.

As I near my sixtieth birthday, I look back to those difficult moments for my mother when she didn't want to let go. Inevitably, I now put myself in the same position. I couldn't let my three children go. I don't have to; wherever I am, whatever I do, they will always be with me.

At this stage in my life, it is playing the roles of a good dad – and husband, son, brother and friend – that are amongst the most fulfilling for me, even if they aren't always as interesting to the outside world. I've also come to realise that they are the roles that would have made my mother most proud.

Yes, I am the sum of these parts. They are all me and through my children I have found myself.

And I'll never let go.

POSTSCRIPT

By the way, I have solved my problems with New Year's Eve –
by marrying Rosemarie Ford on 31 December 2006!

TELEVISION, FILM AND THEATRE

TELEVISION
The Roses of Eyam, 1971
Letter From a Soldier, 1972
Get Some In, 1975-1977
Citizen Smith, 1977-1980
Twelfth Night, 1980
A Midsummer Night's Dream, 1981
All's Well That Ends Well, 1981
Seconds Out, 1981-1982
Cymbeline, 1982
Give Us A Break, 1983
King Lear, 1983
Much Ado About Nothing, 1984
Confessional, 1989
Nightingales, 1990-1993
GBH, 1991
Genghis Cohn, 1993
The Wimbledon Poisoner, 1994
Jake's Progress, 1995
The Office, 1996
Brazen Hussies, 1996
Goodbye My Love, 1996
Hornblower, 1998-1999
The Canterbury Tales, 1998-2000

Oliver Twist, 1999
My Family, 2000-present
Don't Eat the Neighbours, 2001
Hawk, 2001
Jericho, 2005
Friends and Crocodiles, 2005
A Very Social Secretary, 2005
Gideon's Daughter, 2005
Who Do You Think You Are?, 2006
Extras II, 2006
The Trial of Tony Blair, 2007

FILM
That'll Be the Day, 1973
Three For All, 1975
Bert Rigby, You're a Fool, 1989
Strike it Rich (UK)/Loser Takes All (US), 1990
Fierce Creatures, 1997
Remember Me, 1997
Divorcing Jack, 1998
Wimbledon, 2004

THEATRE
The Roses of Eyam, 1970
Julius Caesar, 1971
Cornish Passion Play, 1971
Guys and Dolls, 1971
Journey's End, 1972
Narrow Road to the Deep North, 1972
Godspell, 1973

A Bequest to the Nation, 1974
The Changeling, 1975
Leaping Ginger, 1979
The Lower Depths, 1980
The Three Musketeers, 1980
Trelawny of the Wells, 1981
The Cherry Orchard, 1981
Beaux Strategem, 1982
How I Got That Story, 1982
Philoctetes, 1982
Hamlet, 1983
Me and My Girl (UK), 1984-1985
Me and My Girl (US), 1986-1987
Becket, 1992
Cyrano de Bergerac, 1993
Richard III, 1996
Oliver!, 1997
Power, 2005
The Entertainer, 2007
Aristo, 2008

INDEX

CREDITS

PHOTOGRAPHS

Front cover © Sina Essary
1-12, 16, 19, 27, 33, 34, 44-46, 49,
61, 65, 66, 72, 76, 77 and back cover
© Robert Lindsay
13 © J.F. Coy
14 © J. Lally
17 © New College Nottingham
20 © J. Sims
21, 58 © BBC
22 © Richard Sadler
24 © Western Morning News
Back cover flap, 28, 40-42, 69-71,
74, 75, 78-81, page 271 © Rex
Features Ltd
29 © Dick James Productions
30, 31, 55, 56 © FremantleMedia
38 © Kevin Cummins
43 and end papers © Mirrorpix
50, 51 © Warner Bros.
52 original © Millimeter Films
53 © Channel 4 Television
54, 59, 60, 67, 68 © Nobby Clark
57, 63 © Estate of Ivan Kyncl
62, 64 © Paul Rider
73 © Charlie Gray

OTHER CREDITS

Page 8 © May Sarton, lines taken
from *Journal of a Solitude*
Page 92 'Young and Beautiful', Abner
Silver, Aaron Schroeder
© Schroeder International LLC
Page 93 'Vincent', Don McLean
© Hal Leonard Corporation
Page 126 *The Entertainer*
© John Osborne, first published by
Faber & Faber 1957

*Every effort has been made to trace and
acknowledge the owners of the various
pieces of material in this publication. If
further proof of ownership should be made
available then attribution will be given,
or if requested the said material removed,
in any subsequent editions.*